The 5 Ingredient

Plant-Powered Cookbook

for College Students

100+ Whole Food, Budget-Friendly Vegan Recipes for Quick Meal Prepping to Nourish the Body and Thrive Through Higher Education

Silvana Siskov

Thank you for purchasing
The 5 Ingredient Plant-Powered Cookbook
for College Students

As a special thank you for purchasing this book,

go to bit.ly/vegan-on-the-go

and download a free bonus

"Vegan on the Go: The Ultimate No-Cook Meal Ideas
for Busy Weeks"

THE 5 INGREDIENT PLANT-POWERED COOKBOOK FOR COLLEGE STUDENTS

www.silvanasiskov.com

Limits of Liability and Disclaimer of Warranty

The author and publisher shall not be liable for your misuse of the enclosed material. This book is strictly for informational and educational purposes only.

Warning Disclaimer

The purpose of this book is to educate and entertain. The author and/or publisher shall have neither liability nor responsibility to anyone with respect to any loss or damage caused or alleged to be caused, directly or indirectly, by the information contained in this book.

Medical Disclaimer

The medical or health information in this book is provided as an information resource only and is not to be used or relied on for diagnostic or treatment purposes. This information is not intended to be patient education, does not create any patient-physician relationship, and should not be used as a substitute for professional diagnosis and treatment.

Table of Contents

Introduction

Welcome to *The 5 Ingredient Plant-Powered Cookbook for College Students.*

Whether you're an established vegan or just curious about plant-based living and its health benefits, this book will be a great companion on your journey to fuel your body and mind.

You're probably well aware of the many advantages of a vegan diet; it can help lower the risks of increased blood pressure, obesity, and chronic diseases like diabetes and heart issues.

But apart from the physical benefits, a vegan diet is also known for supporting mental health and keeping you less anxious and stressed. It can also improve your mental focus, which is so important during your college years while trying to meet the demands of the hectic student schedules and long study hours. The benefits of a plant-powered diet are far-reaching, supporting your overall performance and helping you to make the most of your college experience.

This phase of your life represents a transition into independence. For many young people like you, this transition can come with some real challenges, such as moving away from your family home, feeling homesick, juggling coursework and a part-time job, and adapting to a new living and learning environment. That's why prioritising a healthy lifestyle and embracing a wholefood diet that fuels your mind and body is the way to go.

In this book, you will find 100+ whole-food and budget-friendly vegan recipes that are easy to prepare and incredibly nourishing. They will give you an excellent kickstart as you embark on this chapter of your life. The meals are packed with various fruits and vegetables, legumes, nuts, and seeds, providing your body with what it needs to thrive and grow.

Designed to equip you with the knowledge and tools for making nutritious food choices, this book ensures that your college years are academically rewarding and a time of feeling amazing and staying healthy.

Focusing on recipes with only five ingredients or less, this book will be your perfect companion for your college adventure, helping you be successful in your studies while keeping your health and productivity at an optimum level. You'll discover you don't need a long ingredient list to make delicious and nourished dishes. Plant-powered eating can give your body what it needs, even with just a handful of ingredients per meal.

To get the most out of this book, I suggest reading it from the beginning instead of jumping straight into the recipes. Whether you're a master chef or a total beginner in the kitchen, this book offers more than just recipes. It equips you with essential skills and knowledge in and outside the kitchen. You'll learn how to save money on groceries, plan your vegan meals, and easily handle eating in social situations.

The vegan world is where vibrant flavours of foods and natural ingredients come together, crafting nourishing meals that supercharge your body.

Let's dive into the challenges and rewards of vegan college life and embrace a plant-powered lifestyle for a healthier and more vibrant you.

Chapter 1:

Introduction to Vegan Living

"A vegan diet is one of the best things you can do for your health and the well-being of our planet."

- Robert Cheeke

Understanding the Principles of Veganism

Veganism strictly prohibits using animal products, such as dairy, honey, eggs, meat, poultry, fish, and their byproducts. This includes animal-derived fabrics like wool or silk, fur, leather, and suede, products tested on animals, and personal care products containing animal ingredients like lanolin, keratin, beeswax, etc.

Many people decide to go vegan for health reasons, but veganism is not only linked to food choices. It has a strong connection to people's values.

Vegans avoid any form of entertainment that exploits animals for profit, including rodeos, marine parks, roadside zoos, and circuses. They are also against any form of animal maltreatment, such as chaining dogs and cat declawing.

Studies show that each vegan saves about one animal daily through lifestyle choices. [1] This staggering statistic highlights how much power we have with the food choices we make and how vegans make our planet a better place.

Besides caring about animals, being vegan is also about looking after our planet. Raising animals for food is associated with various environmental problems, including air pollution and the release of harmful emissions from factory farms into our water systems. Veganism aims to reduce our excessive use of water, land, and fossil fuels.

Here's a mind-blowing fact: Research done in 2013 showed that raising our crops for people to eat instead of feeding farmed animals, could feed an additional 4 billion people. [2]

That means that going vegan might be a way to reduce world poverty and address environmental problems.

So, while some think that veganism is a new concept centred around not eating animals, it is actually a way of living that stretches beyond the plate.

To fully embrace the benefits of a vegan lifestyle without unnecessary stress, it is important to grasp veganism's fundamental values and principles and learn how to create a well-balanced eating plan.

The most common question that people ask when encountering veganism is, "What do vegans eat?" and the answer is, "A large variety of foods."

A vegan diet offers many options, from vegan sausages to plant-based milk and cheese and numerous other vegan products, allowing you to transform virtually any recipe into a vegan culinary delight.

Here's a comprehensive list of foods you can enjoy without compromising your beliefs and values:

- A variety of fruits and vegetables

- Nuts and seeds

- Non-dairy milk and dairy alternatives, such as vegan butter, coffee creamers, and coconut ice cream

- Non-dairy milk chocolate

- Beans and legumes, like lentils and chickpeas

- All-time favourite carbohydrates: pasta, bread, wraps, bagels, and pitas

- Meat alternatives like deli sandwich slices, veggie burgers, tempeh bacon, and more

- Even indulgent treats like fries, pizzas, onion rings, and cookies are part of a vegan menu

College students must often stick to a budget; a plant-based diet is cost-effective. Foods like beans, lentils, rice, and vegetables are usually cheaper than animal products. This makes a plant-focused diet a smart option for those with little money. Also, it comes with a number of health benefits.

This book serves as your college life food guide, giving you plenty of tips and ideas to enjoy your vegan journey.

In the next section, we'll dive deep into the most essential nutrients for your body and mind, enabling you to flourish and thrive during your college years.

Essential Nutrients in a Vegan Diet

You have already discovered some fantastic health benefits of a vegan diet, but there's a potential problem when you switch to an all-plant diet. This can sometimes mean that you miss out on some essential nutrients your body craves. That's why it's super important to know these essential nutrients that keep your body healthy.

In this section, I'll list foods that contain these essential nutrients and make your body healthy and happy. These foods help you build a balanced diet that boosts your energy, sharpens your focus, and keeps you feeling at your best.

Vitamin B12

B12 supports your nervous system and is a crucial vitamin in producing red blood cells, which carry oxygen throughout your body. However, B12 is mainly found in meat. Finding it in plant foods can be a bit like a treasure hunt, but there's good news. Look for B12-fortified plant milk, meat alternatives, breakfast cereal, and nutritional yeast. Some people who follow a vegan diet take daily B12 supplements for that extra energy boost.

Iron

Iron is like the engine that keeps your body running smoothly, especially when it comes to carrying oxygen around your body.

There are two kinds of iron in food: non-heme (from plants) and heme (from animal products). The body finds it hard to absorb non-heme iron, but don't worry, you can get your iron fix from plant-based foods like beans, spinach, lentils, seeds, chickpeas, quinoa, dried fruits, and even dark chocolate.

Here is an interesting fact: include vitamin C-rich foods in your meals, like oranges, grapefruit, lemon, kiwis, or veggies such as Brussels sprouts, broccoli, cauliflower, and cabbage. Pairing these vitamin C-rich foods can improve iron absorption and keep energy levels up.

Protein

Protein is like the superhero that keeps your body going, ensuring everything runs smoothly. Some people believe that being vegan means missing out on protein, but that's not true at all. Most vegans get enough, and often, they get even more than they need.

Vegans have many protein-packed choices like seeds, nuts, tofu, and legumes, including lentils and beans. The best thing is that these protein-packed plant foods also come with fibre. This fibre supports digestion, keeps your heart healthy, and reduces the risk of type 2 diabetes. So, whether you're enjoying a bowl of vegetable soup or have a plate of chickpea curry, you're giving your body the superhero fuel it needs.

Calcium

Calcium helps to keep your bones, teeth, and muscles strong and healthy. The best-known sources of calcium can be found in dairy products. But there are amazing vegan-friendly sources, too. You can increase calcium intake with fortified products like almond butter, black beans, broccoli, and kale. Another option to get calcium in your diet is from tofu, set with calcium salts. So, whether you're enjoying almond butter toast or a yummy tofu stir-fry, your body is still getting the calcium it needs.

Fats

There are two kinds of fat – good and bad, or healthy and unhealthy. The good fat helps your body to store energy and keeps you healthy. You will find them in walnuts, chia seeds, flaxseeds, olive oil, and avocado. Some people also supplement with algae oil to supercharge their essential fats.

Vitamin C

Vitamin C protects your cells from free radicals. Vegans usually get their vitamin C from eating tons of fruits. As mentioned earlier, vitamin C is also vital for iron absorption. Some of the best sources of vitamin C include oranges, grapefruit, Brussels sprouts, strawberries, blackcurrants, kale, spring greens, mango, and broccoli.

Vitamin D

Vitamin D takes care of your bones and your immune system. It also controls your mood and muscle recovery, and it helps the body to absorb calcium better. Vitamin D deficiency is a problem for both meat-eaters and vegans. Some vegans take vegan vitamin D supplements. The best and easiest way to get vitamin D into your body is to spend at least 30 minutes a day outside enjoying the sun. This will do wonders for your health. But make sure that you protect your skin by using a sunscreen or wearing a hat.

Vitamin A

Vitamin A is usually found in animal sources, but our bodies can turn beta carotene (a reddish-orange pigment present in a variety of fresh fruits and vegetables) into vitamin A. Eating foods high in beta carotene, such as carrots and sweet potatoes, along with some healthy fat, can improve this conversion.

To create a balanced vegan diet, I recommend you include a variety of plant-based foods in your eating plan. Think of it like a rainbow - each colour provides your body with different nutrients, allowing you to experience optimum health.

Meeting the Nutritional Needs of the Body

In the previous section, you learned that creating a well-balanced meal plan is vital for meeting your nutritional needs. With that knowledge, you're better equipped to fill the dietary gaps when creating your meal plan.

Here are a few tips on how to meet your nutritional needs without stress. Remember, it's okay to treat yourself now and then:

Plan Your Meals

Planning your meals will help you get all the nutrients you need, and it's the cheapest way to ensure you don't exceed your budget. Ordering unhealthy and expensive takeaways is very easy if you don't plan your meals. I get it; humans strive for convenience, but remember that meal planning leads to healthy and wallet-friendly eating.

Load Your Diet with Fruit and Vegetables

Fruit and vegetables make a plant-based diet vibrant and delicious. A diverse choice of fruits and vegetables full of nutrients and antioxidants are excellent calcium and vitamin C sources. Deep yellow and orange fruits and vegetables, like carrots and squash, help meet many of your daily vitamin needs.

Enjoy Grains

The healthiest options in this food group are whole grains like quinoa, brown rice, and whole wheat bread since they're high in fibre and include zinc and iron.

Consider Soy Products and Beans

Beans are packed with protein, iron, potassium, and fibre. Soy products, such as tempeh, tofu and soy milk, are loaded with high-quality protein. Soy and beans are also excellent sources of isoflavones, which are known for lowering the risk of cancer. You can also use canned beans, which are more convenient and cheaper than regular beans, but the nutritional content is similar.

Snack on Nuts and Seeds

Despite being high in calories, nuts and seeds are rich in nutrients. They are full of fibre, minerals and healthy fats. Lots of studies have found a connection between nuts and heart health. So, make sure you always have a bag of nuts with you. If hunger strikes, you're well prepared with this nutrient-rich option.

Choose Wholefoods

Unlike processed foods, wholefoods are minimally processed and contain more nutrients. In addition to being unhealthy, processed foods are not always the cheapest option.

Lower Saturated Fat Intake

Vegans don't need to worry about saturated fat because it comes mainly from animal products. However, I suggest you keep an eye on the number of processed foods you eat, as they often contain palm oil, which is high in saturated fat, and contributes to unhealthy cholesterol and triglycerides that cause heart disease.

Stay Hydrated

Water helps break down food, dissolves nutrients, and helps deliver vitamin components to the rest of the body. Staying hydrated increases concentration and decreases mental fatigue. As a college student, feeling fatigue, dizziness, and poor concentration are the last things you want to experience, especially during exams. My best tip to stay hydrated throughout the day is to carry a water bottle wherever you go.

Remember, taking care of your body is an ongoing journey. Be open to experimenting with different vegan ingredients to get the most out of your food. Your body will thank you for it!

Before we go further with the book, I want to highlight something important. A vegan diet is a healthy diet only if you choose to eat natural or whole foods. Bingeing on junk foods, such as vegan pizzas, cookies, plant-based ice cream, and other processed snacks, is not a healthy alternative to eating processed meat products.

Chapter 2:

Vegan Cooking and Meal Planning

"Good food is very often, even most often, simple food."

- Anthony Bourdain

Basic Cooking Techniques for Beginners

Cooking is about bringing out the best flavours from your ingredients. If you have some cooking experience, you'll know there are various cooking techniques, and each one brings a different flavour to the same ingredient.

So, before you start cooking your meals, let's talk about some of these cooking methods:

Sautéing

This is a quick and easy way to cook veggies. Heat a small amount of oil or fat in a shallow pan, and stir-fry chopped vegetables quickly over a high heat until they are tender. You can add various seasonings and sauces for different flavours.

Steaming

Steaming is great for keeping the nutrients in vegetables. All you need is to add a bit of water to the saucepan (about ⅓ full) and bring the water to the boil. Put veggies in a steamer basket and place this inside the saucepan, suspended over the boiling water. Reduce the heat of the saucepan so that the water gently bubbles. Remove the vegetables when they are tender, then serve.

Grilling

Brush veggies with olive or vegetable oil and sprinkle with your favourite seasoning, then put them under the hot preheated grill. This will add a smoky flavour to your vegan creations.

Simmering

Simmering is the cooking method used for making soups and stews. Add your favourite vegetables with legumes, seasonings, and a well-flavoured vegetable broth to a large saucepan. Bring to the boil, cover the pan with a lid, and reduce the heat so that the liquid is gently bubbling. Cook until the vegetables are soft when pierced with a fork. This type of food is ideal for batch cooking and freezing, so you always have it ready when you're short of time.

Roasting

Roasted vegetables are my favourite. This method brings out the natural sweetness. Roasting is suitable for most vegetables, but root vegetables like potatoes, carrots and parsnips are the best. Preheat a deep baking tray containing a few tablespoons of cooking or olive oil in the middle of the oven. Remove the tin from the oven and very carefully add the vegetables, spooning a little of the vegetable oil over them. When they become golden and tender (about 45 minutes to 1 hour), they are ready to eat.

Boiling

This is the simplest way of cooking and is perfect for pasta and rice. All you need to do is half-fill the saucepan with lightly salted water and follow the cooking instructions on the packaging. The instructions usually tell you to wait for the water to boil before adding the food. Reduce the heat, so that the water is gently bubbling and cook the rice/pasta for the time indicated on the packet. Stir both gently with a fork to avoid clumping. Taste the food to ensure that it is cooked before removing the pan from the heat and draining well. Add a knob of butter and mix gently into the rice or pasta before serving. *Flora Original* is suitable for vegans and is perfect for cooking.

If you're new to cooking, you're probably overwhelmed by the idea of prepping and cooking. However, learning these simple basic cooking techniques will boost your confidence and help you develop excellent cooking skills to prepare something tasty without all the fuss.

Secrets to Quick Meal Preparation

Meal prepping is often overrated and is considered to be time-consuming. But in reality, it doesn't need to take too much of your time; it can be done in advance, and prepared ingredients can be kept in the refrigerator until needed.

In this section, I'll show you some quick meal-prepping secrets to help you enjoy your time in the kitchen:

Have a Recipe List Planned

To fuel your body with various foods, instead of settling for the same old, I suggest having a list of quick recipes handy that use different types of food. You'll find plenty of these recipes later in the book.

Substitute

When following recipes, don't forget to look at alternatives if you are missing an ingredient. If the recipe suggests you use an ingredient that you can't find or cannot afford, swap it with something similar. Also, many dishes are still delicious, even if you remove one of the ingredients completely from the recipe.

Prep for the Week

If you have some free time at the weekends, prepare a few meals for the week ahead and store them in the fridge or freezer. Also, cooking large portions of grains or vegetables can save you time and money. It's a perfect way for quick and easy meal prepping for the week ahead, as the vegetables will go well with most dishes and add plenty of nutrition to your plate.

Cook in Bulk

Occasionally, I suggest you cook large batches of your favourite foods, portion them, and freeze them. This will save you time during busy days and exams. It's a real money and time saver and a great way to reduce the temptation for expensive takeaways or junk food.

Keep Things Simple

When time is tight, keep everything simple. Choose one-pot recipes like curry or lentil stew for quick cooking and minimal washing of dishes. These types of meals are ideal for bulk cooking and freezing. If kept in the freezer, you can cook just once but eat it many times over the next few weeks or months.

Multi-Task

Saving time is the name of the game in speedy meal prep. Multitasking teaches you to use your time wisely. Cook lentils or quinoa on the stovetop, while at the same time, you can roast or bake granola or sweet potatoes in the oven. Or you can bake cookies in the oven while making salad dressings. With a bit of multitasking, you can prepare several meals within an hour.

Chop and Freeze

Preparing ingredients in advance is always a great idea if you like freshly cooked meals and don't want to eat Sunday's soup on Wednesday! Chop the vegetables you'll use in your meals and freeze them. You can do this once or twice a month if you have enough space in the freezer. Not only will you save time when cooking, but you'll also prevent the vegetables in your fridge from going to waste.

DIY Your Smoothies

Putting all the smoothie ingredients in a freezer bag can be a time saver when you need a quick breakfast or snack. All you have to do is blend them with the liquid of your choice.

With these tips and an extensive list of recipes from this book, you'll be well-equipped to create a healthy meal plan that doesn't overstretch your budget.

Meal Planning Strategies

Using campus dining rooms or cafes instead of taking in your home-prepared foods might seem more convenient, but it's undoubtedly more expensive.

While fast food can save you time, it can affect your budget! Remember, it is best to make a healthy meal at home. So, put away your suffering wallet and learn some meal-planning strategies. Sticking to your budget is crucial in college life.

Here are four simple steps to follow:

1. Before you begin meal planning and shopping, you must look through your fridge, freezer, and kitchen cupboards. It'll only take a few minutes to inspect your kitchen thoroughly to ensure you know what foods you have so you can avoid buying unnecessary duplicates.

2. Once that's done, list what foods you have. You must check the expiration dates on your food items and decide which ones should be used first. This will help you prevent food waste and save money.

3. Plan your meals and snacks around the foods you already have at home. Then, decide what you want each day for breakfast, lunch, dinner, and snacks making sure that you're including plenty of nutrition in each meal. Don't just make a mental note of it; write it down. Take a blank piece of paper or open a document on your computer and write down the meals you want to eat on each day of the week. This will prevent you from overeating and going over your budget.

In the second part of this book, you'll find over 100 recipes that will give you plenty of ideas to include in your meal plans. Try to coincide your shopping with the time your local supermarket reduces its prices on fresh produce, and watch out for reduced-priced veggie boxes.

Here's a table to help you with your weekly meal plan.

WEEKLY MEAL PLAN							
Meals	MON	TUE	WED	THU	FRI	SAT	SUN
Dinner							
Lunch							
Breakfast							
Snack							
Tasks to prepare for tomorrow							

The table includes a row 'Tasks to prepare for tomorrow.' This could include removing food from the freezer the night before or pre-cutting fruits for your morning smoothie.

In this chapter, you've discovered various cooking techniques to help you bring out the best flavours from your food; you have also learned quick meal-prepping secrets and meal-planning strategies to save you time and money.

In the next chapter, we'll explore how to make the most of your budget while shopping for ingredients. Combining shopping tactics and meal planning skills, you can enjoy healthier, home-cooked meals even during your busiest college days.

Chapter 3:

Grocery Shopping and Budgeting

"Used correctly, a budget doesn't restrict you; it empowers you."

- Tere Stouffer

Budget-Friendly Shopping

As a college student, mastering the art of budgeting is a crucial skill. Effectively managing your food expenses can pay off big time. Here are some practical tips that can help you make your food shopping affordable and nutritious:

Set a Budget

Decide how much you can afford to spend on food each week and stick to it. Be realistic. Sometimes, it might be hard not to go over the budget, but here is my tip – write everything down. When I was younger and didn't have much money, I remember writing down every time I spent some money, no matter how small, I kept writing everything down. That kept me disciplined and helped me not to overspend. When you know where your money is going, you can make better choices about your spending.

Create a Shopping List

Once you've decided on your budget, it's time to create a meal plan.

Earlier in the book, you learned how to plan your meals for a week. After creating a meal plan, list all the groceries you'll need for it and take a list with you when shopping.

To make a grocery list even more effective, divide it into sections such as fruit and vegetables, grains, drinks, frozen foods, canned goods, etc. It'll save you time in the shop as most items from the same group are placed together.

Shop Smart

Here are a few things to remember to keep your grocery bill low:

- Stock up on sale items. Look for sales and discounts

- Choose generic brands instead of big-name brands: Generic or store-branded products are often cheaper and just as good quality.

- If you use a particular item often, consider buying in bulk: Buying a bag of vegetables is less expensive than buying only a few pieces. This applies to most items.

- Avoid buying on campus (on-campus stores often have higher prices): Explore supermarkets outside of campus.

- Snack before shopping (or, even better, have a well-balanced meal): When you're hungry, your stomach becomes bigger than your eyes, and you might buy items that you don't need or reach for junk food.

- Stick to your list and budget: Take your grocery list when going shopping, and don't buy anything that's not on it.

- Stock up on tinned beans and vegetables when on sale: Take advantage of this, as these items have a long shelf life and can be stored for several years.

- Check expiry dates: Always check expiration dates before purchasing and buy products with a longer shelf life.

Timing Matters

Many large shops discount foods an hour or two before closing time. That's the perfect time to go shopping. Some produce may be reduced to half price or more if their expiry date ends soon. If you buy items with a short shelf life, consume them on the same day or store them in the freezer as soon as you get home.

Think About Cost, Not Convenience

Products focused on convenience are often pricey and will make your budget go haywire. Of course, buying pre-chopped vegetables is convenient, but they often cost more. Purchasing whole vegetables and slicing them yourself will be cheaper and fresher.

Shop at Farmer's Market

Buying food at a farmer's market is often cheaper than in local food stores. The food from these markets is also much fresher and locally sourced.

Buy Seasonal Food

If you're on a very tight budget, look for seasonal recipes or plan your meals around fruits and vegetables that are in season. They tend to be cheaper.

Avoid Uncommon Ingredients

When searching for recipes online, avoid those that call for unique or uncommon ingredients. They're often more expensive. To keep your costs down, I suggest you opt for recipes that use more affordable ingredients and those that you'll use repeatedly.

Shop Online

Shopping online can save you time and money. It'll help you stick to your grocery list and not buy things you don't need or buy more than you need to.

Look for Budget-Friendly Protein Sources

Choose budget-friendly protein sources, such as beans, tofu, or lentils, instead of plant-based protein powders. They are nutritious and more cost-effective.

Freeze

Freezing food is a great way to prevent waste and extend shelf life. Many foods, including breads, fruits, and vegetables, freeze well and can be kept for up to six months.

You Don't Need to Buy in Bulk

Don't buy food in large packages you don't use. Strict rule – don't buy ingredients that you will use only once. This can lead to waste and unnecessary expenses.

Get Creative in the Kitchen

Use your imagination to prevent food waste. It can save you lots of money. Consider doing the following:

- Purchase foods that you can include in several meals throughout the week.

- Use stale bread to make croutons or toast.

- Don't throw away wilted vegetables. Soak them in ice water for 5-10 minutes to bring them back to life. If you can't save them, use them to cook a stew or soup and then freeze it.

- Have overripe avocado? Blend it into a green smoothie or chocolate mousse.

Implementing these practical tips will help you control your grocery shopping and positively impact your finances. It can add up over time, even if you only save a little money each week. With some planning and smart shopping, you'll make your food budget work for you.

Tips for Batch Cooking and Freezing

Juggling coursework, social activities, and maybe even a part-time job, may mean that you do not find you have much time for cooking.

Batch cooking and freezing are the way to go when you are short of time. It'll make your life easier, healthier, and it's more budget friendly. This strategy will be very convenient during your exams or when you must grab a quick meal between classes.

I remember doing this when I was a student. I didn't do any cooking during exam time, but I still ate healthy meals every day because I had pre-cooked food in the freezer.

Many people see batch cooking as a lifesaver. I want to show you how bulk cooking can also be a timesaver. Here are some tips to make bulk cooking easy and simple:

Cook Large Portions

Cook a large amount of food when you have time. Instead of cooking a single portion, cook enough foods that can serve several meals. Invest time now to see the rewards later.

Dishes like soups, stews, sauces, etc., can be cooked and stored in the freezer.

Make a habit of cooking large batches of food you enjoy that can be stored in the freezer. Doing it only once a week or once a month can help you save lots of time later.

Portion and Freeze

Once cooked, divide the dish into small portions and freeze them for later use. Doing this will ensure you always have meals ready. This will save you time and money. Batch cooking also helps you control the serving size and minimise food waste.

Cook a Variety of Foods

Make sure you always have a variety of dishes in the freezer to have a varied choice. This will help you maintain a balanced diet and enjoy a variety of dishes without cooking daily.

Think of Convenience

Batch cooking is all about simplicity and convenience. It's like having a takeaway, but it's a much healthier alternative and more cost-effective. You only need to take the food out of the freezer and heat it up.

Save Time and Money

Batch cooking is known as a time and money saver. You only cook food once but eat it many times later. Therefore, it saves you time and helps you save on utility bills. Also, buying many ingredients often comes at a reduced price. I suggest you take advantage of it and cook a large meal.

I hope I've successfully shown you the benefits of batch cooking. This culinary strategy is simple to implement with a bit of planning. So, give it a try. It's a great habit to develop.

Must-Have Kitchen Tools and Utensils

Students don't need many fancy kitchen gadgets. If you live in rented accommodation, your kitchen will probably have the most essential items, such as saucepans and frying pans. However, there are a few must-have kitchen tools and utensils that can simplify vegan cooking and make it quick and easy:

Blender

Ask your family members to gift you one if you can't afford to purchase it for yourself. Or add it to your Christmas or birthday wish list. A high-speed blender works better and faster than the standard one. It can blend even tough ingredients like frozen bananas or nuts. They are perfect for making smoothies, creamy soups, and salad dressings. If you're on a tight budget, a standard blender will also be helpful in your kitchen.

Non-Stick Sauté Pan

A non-stick sauté pan is tall and has straight sides. This prevents spillages. It's ideal for sautéing vegetables, making tofu scramble, or cooking veggie-loaded pasta sauce.

Sharp Knife

It's always better to purchase one expensive sharp knife than several cheap knives. A good knife can last a lifetime, making chopping and dicing easy.

Cutting Board

Vegans spend lots of time cutting and chopping vegetables. Therefore, a cutting board is essential for preparing your ingredients efficiently.

Non-Stick Frying Pan

A non-stick frying pan is versatile and can be used for cooking a wide range of vegan meals, including stir-fries, veggies, tofu, veggie burgers, pancakes, and more.

Mixing Bowls

A set of mixing bowls is a must-have. They are versatile; you can make salad, batter, and other meal preparations.

Glass Food Storage Containers and Jars

These are fantastic for storing leftovers, keeping pre-chopped veggies fresh, or preparing single-serving meals for lunch or dinner.

Baking Dishes or Trays

Having at least one baking tray or dish for oven-cooked meals is a good idea. While non-stick versions are ideal, you can also choose the budget-friendly options made from glass, ceramic, or stainless steel.

Measuring Cups and Spoons

When following recipes, you will need measuring cups and spoons. They ensure your meals turn out perfectly, preventing food waste from poorly cooked dishes.

Reusable Food Containers

These containers are a must-have for storing food in the fridge or kitchen cupboards and are perfect for storing leftovers efficiently.

These kitchen utensils will make your cooking easier and more enjoyable, whether preparing quick meals or tackling complex recipes. Most of these kitchen tools are practical and inexpensive, allowing you to enjoy the process of cooking while creating delicious vegan meals.

Chapter 4:

Eating Out and About

"Being vegan keeps my body fuelled and running smoothly."

- *Madelaine Petsch*

Navigating Campus Dining and Social Events

Eating on campus and navigating social events shouldn't be too much of a problem. Many places that sell foods understand the various dietary requirements and are becoming more accommodating to their customers' needs.

Even though veganism is becoming increasingly popular, and it's getting easier to adopt a vegan lifestyle, vegan students may still face unique challenges compared to their non-vegan friends. Let's look at some of the challenges you might experience as a vegan student:

Cooking in the Dorm

I understand that you may not be able to prepare extravagant dishes if your access to the kitchen is limited, but you can still make things work with some basic equipment. A microwave, a mini-fridge, and a small electric hot plate hob will allow you to cook various dishes, including most of the recipes in this book. So, you can enjoy delicious vegan meals even in a dorm.

Campus Dining Rooms

As global awareness of veganism continues to rise, many campuses have vegan menus and options. If you're unhappy about the vegan options available, don't hesitate to approach the dining staff and give them your feedback and suggestions tailored to your dietary needs. Your input can contribute to changes and improve things for you and other vegan students.

Restaurants and Cafes

Nowadays, many eating places have vegan menus, plant-based dishes, or dishes that can be adjusted to vegan preferences. Also, many high streets and college towns provide a choice of diverse restaurants and cafes, including Indian, Chinese, pizza, and vegan establishments.

Attending Social Events

Attending any social event can be challenging if you have limited dietary requirements. This does not include only vegans but also people following various diets such as vegetarian, halal, gluten-free, dairy-free, sugar-free, and more. That's why preparation is the key. You can eat before the event, bring your food and snacks to share with others, or speak to the host and let them know your food preferences. You always have a choice. So, make sure you always feel comfortable during social gatherings.

Social Pressure

Your morals and values are important to you and make you who you are. However, staying true to yourself could be challenging when facing peer pressure. Vegan philosophy is unfamiliar to some people, and if you live in shared accommodation with other students or flatmates who are not vegans, it could lead to potential conflicts in the kitchen. In such situations, I suggest requesting a separate kitchen cupboard or the shelf in the fridge for your exclusive use. This way, you can avoid sharing dishes, food, or kitchen tools with others, helping you maintain harmony in shared living spaces.

Eating Out on a Budget

When dining out on a limited budget, you can implement a few smart strategies to make your experience budget-friendly and your meals delicious. A helpful tip that I can give you includes exploring *Side Orders*. Most menus have this section. These side dishes usually contain a variety of vegetables and salads. They often cost a fraction of the price of a main meal. Ordering two side dishes is often much cheaper than ordering a single main dish.

In this section of the book, I provide various options and tactics to help you successfully manage your eating-out experience as a vegan. By incorporating these ideas into your daily life, you can better manage your student budget while enjoying your vegan experience. The key is to be proactive.

Meal Prepping and Eating Tips for Busy Weeks

College life is filled with a mixture of busy and less hectic times. During those demanding weeks, planning is the key.

You're most likely to settle for convenience food and takeaways during such a period, but they are more expensive and less healthy. These choices won't benefit your health or help your budget.

As discussed earlier, meal planning and smart budgeting go hand in hand. Meal planning will not only keep you healthy but will also help you budget wisely.

Here are a few tips that I'd like to share with you:

Meal Prepping and Batch Cooking

I've mentioned this several times before and highlighted its importance. During less busy times, I recommend preparing meals for your busy days, or cooking large batches that you can store in the fridge or freezer for later use.

Smoothies

Smoothies are my favourite type of breakfast for busy mornings. They are lifesavers. They are not only quick and easy to prepare, but they are also packed with essential nutrients. Add fruits, seeds, nuts, or veggies like spinach or kale. You'll find a few smoothie recipes in this book.

I often prepare all the ingredients the night before. You can also use frozen fruits from the freezer. In the morning, all you need to do is to put everything in the blender and turn the switch on. If you're tight on time, you can make a smoothie the night before and store it in the fridge so it's ready to grab and rush through the door.

Smoothies are a fantastic student-friendly breakfast option for those busy mornings.

Overnight Oats

This is another great option for a busy lifestyle. Just as the name suggests, you prepare them the night before. So, it doesn't matter how rushed your mornings are. I have included the recipe in this book.

Roasted Vegetables

I love them. Not only are they delicious, but they are very easy to make. You can place any vegetable on a baking tray with no cooking skills involved. Also, you do other things while the vegetables roast in the oven. When ready, put them in a container and take them with you.

Sandwiches and Wraps

They are quick and convenient to prepare, and you can take them anywhere. They can be made in minutes and are ideal for a light lunch.

Salads

Salad dishes are great for lunch, dinner, or snacks. You can add grains or greens and place them in a container, ready to take out.

Stir-Fries

They offer a quick and satisfying meal. Quickly fry veggies in a non-stick frying pan; you can serve them with rice if you're feeling extra hungry.

Instant Pot Meals

If you have access to the kitchen with an instant pot, it can significantly reduce the cooking time for your soups and stews so you can enjoy it during your busiest days.

Meal Prep in Mason Jars

A Mason jar is a glass used for canning and preserving food. It has a glass or metal lid and a threaded ring. This ensures an airtight seal, preserving the freshness and quality of the food stored inside. They are particularly beneficial for busy students as they are compact and easy to carry. They can be used for a variety of foods, are easy to clean, and are ideal for advance food prepping and storing. Having several meals prepared in Mason jars is a perfect solution for busy students. They are easy to put together and excellent for eating on the go. You can also prepare them in advance. These meals include overnight oats, salad, soup, various rice dishes, and many more.

One-Pot Meals

A simple way to cook nutritious vegan foods is to put various vegetables into a saucepan and cook them together. It is a very straightforward way to make a healthy vegan meal.

No-Cook Meals

There are many no-cook options, which are excellent choices for busy days or when you're out and about. One convenient option is a non-dairy yoghurt, granola, and seeds combo. It is healthy and simple to prepare.

For more ideas on eating out during a hectic week, visit bit.ly/vegan-on-the-go and download a free bonus, *Vegan on the Go: The Ultimate No-Cook Meal Ideas for Busy Weeks.* This meal plan will help you to enjoy nutritious and delicious meals without the hassle of cooking.

Understanding how to store and reheat your food when you are on the go is crucial, and that's precisely what I'll cover in the next section.

Storage and Reheating Tips

Storing your food correctly will keep your food safe from developing bacteria and reduce food waste. Reheating your meals correctly will ensure that your food tastes great.

Let's dive straight into looking at the best ways to store your foods:

Get Reusable Containers

Getting various sizes of reusable airtight containers is a safe and cheap way to store your food in the fridge and on the go. These containers prevent food from drying out and are suitable for microwave use. Most plastic containers are microwave safe, which means they are convenient for heating and eating while on campus or in a dorm.

Refrigerate Food Only When Cool

Ensure that food is cool before storing it in the fridge. Putting warm or hot food directly in the fridge can raise the temperature of the fridge, leading to bacteria growth.

Label and Date

This is especially useful if you cook a batch and have various dishes in the freezer. Labelling and dating your dishes can be extremely helpful. The most common method is to use masking tape and a marker to write the name of the dish and the preparation date.

Freeze Some of the Foods

Ensure you freeze the food you don't plan to eat immediately or within a few days. Don't forget to use freezer-safe containers or freezer bags and label them appropriately.

Portion

Before storing food, ensure that you divide a dish into smaller portions. This makes reheating easier and reduces food waste. It also helps you to manage your meals more effectively.

Keep Fruit and Vegetables Separately

I recommend you store fruits and vegetables separately from other foods to keep them fresh for longer. Some fruits like apples and bananas release ethylene gas, causing vegetables to ripen faster.

Sealed Containers

If you plan to carry food in your bag, buy sealed containers with a locking mechanism. This will prevent food from spilling.

Now, let's look at some tips for safely reheating your food:

Use a Microwave

This is probably the most common and convenient way of reheating food, whether the food is kept in the fridge, freezer, or containers. Most campus kitchens and dining halls have a microwave available. When reheating foods such as rice, lentils or quinoa, cover them with a damp cloth or a paper towel to hold the moisture in and prevent them from drying out. During reheating in the microwave, don't forget to stir it several times to ensure all food is equally heated. This especially applies to reheating frozen dishes.

Use a Hob

This is another common and practical way of reheating food, particularly for soups and stews. Put the food in the saucepan on medium heat and stir occasionally. Add some water or broth to prevent your dish from drying and sticking to the bottom of the saucepan.

Use a Toaster

Using a toaster is a fast and convenient method for defrosting bread slices quickly.

Use the Oven

Oven reheating suits casseroles, pizzas, and other dishes you may want to crisp up. To reheat the food, the oven temperature should be between 355-375°F (180-190°C). Ensure you place the food in an oven-safe dish and in the middle of the oven and cover it with foil to prevent it from burning and drying out.

Don't Overcook

Whichever reheating method you use, don't overcook it. Your food will be dry and won't taste nice.

Reheat Food Only Once

Reheating foods many times can develop harmful bacteria. Reheat only the portion of the food you're ready to eat.

To make your leftovers or reheated food tastier, add fresh ingredients to it. Adding fresh herbs, sauces, or greens ensures your food will be much more delicious.

Make sure that you follow the tips I've shared with you in this section. These storage and reheating methods will ensure your food is safe and tasty.

So far, you've learned a lot about the vegan lifestyle and cooking. In the next chapter of this book, you'll find 100+ vegan recipes. These recipes will kickstart your day, keep you satisfied, and nourish you throughout the day.

I strongly encourage you to implement what you have learned while preparing these delicious vegan dishes. By doing so, your body and your future self will thank you. Happy cooking!

Lots of love xx

Silvana

Chapter 5:

Recipes for Your Student Vegan Experience

"There are many ways to love your body, but fuelling your body with nutritious food is the highest form of self-respect."

- Ania Drosnes

In this part of the book, you'll discover 100+ vegan recipes to keep your body happy and healthy.

Before experimenting with these recipes, please note that serving sizes vary depending on the recipe. Some recipes are suitable for two or more people. You must always adjust the ingredient quantities accordingly if you cook only for yourself and don't want any leftovers.

Breakfast to Kickstart Your Day

These vegan breakfast recipes will kickstart your day with a bang!

They are packed with nutrients to keep your energy levels up until your next meal. These delicious and convenient recipes are perfect for students seeking healthy vegan breakfast options. Many recipes can be prepared in advance to save you time in the morning.

Berry Banana Smoothie with Nut Butter and Cinnamon [3]

Serving: 1

Ingredients:

- 1 frozen banana
- 1 cup frozen berries (blueberries, strawberries, etc.)
- 1 tablespoon nut butter (almond, peanut, cashew, etc.)
- ¼-½ teaspoon cinnamon
- 1 cup unsweetened non-dairy milk (soy, cashew, almond, etc.)

Instructions:

1. Blend all ingredients until smooth.
2. Add milk or water to achieve the desired thickness.

Peanut Butter Chia Pudding [4]

Servings: 2

Ingredients:

- ¼ cup chia seeds
- 2 tablespoons peanut butter
- 1 cup unsweetened plant-based milk
- 1 tablespoon maple syrup
- ½ teaspoon vanilla

Instructions:

1. In a large mixing bowl, whisk all the ingredients together.
2. Let it sit for 2 minutes, then stir again.
3. Cover the bowl with cling film and refrigerate for at least 4 hours or overnight until it thickens.

Spinach and Tomato Breakfast Wrap [5]

Serving: 1

Ingredients:

- 1 wrap
- ½ cup hummus

- ½ cup spinach
- 3 long slices of tomato
- ¼ cup chopped avocado

Instructions:

1. Spread hummus over the entire wrap.
2. Add the remaining ingredients to the wrap, then roll it up securely.
3. Slice it in half and enjoy.

Berry Nut Butter Overnight Oats [6]

Serving: 1

Ingredients:

- ½ cup old-fashioned oats
- 1 tablespoon nut butter
- 1 teaspoon chia seeds
- ½ cup almond milk
- A handful of fresh berries of your choice

Instructions:

1. Sprinkle oats on the bottom of the jar or other container. Add chia seeds.
2. Pour almond milk and completely cover the oats.
3. Mix well after adding the nut butter.
4. Put the lid on the jar and refrigerate overnight.
5. You can store it for up to five days. You may either reheat the oatmeal or eat it cold.
6. Top with fresh berries before serving.

Banana Oat Pancakes [7]

Servings: 6 pancakes

Ingredients:

- 1 cup oatmeal
- 1 ripe banana
- ½ cup almond milk
- 1 teaspoon baking powder
- 2 tablespoons maple syrup

Instructions:

1. Blend all the ingredients until smooth.
2. Add oil to a large non-stick pan or griddle over medium heat.
3. Cook pancakes for approximately 2-3 minutes until golden brown on both sides.
4. Continue until there is no more batter.

Vegan Blueberry Muffins [8]

Servings: 6

Ingredients:

- 1 banana
- 1 cup quinoa (cooked)
- ¼ cup vegan Greek yoghurt
- ¼ cup almond butter
- 1 cup blueberries

Instructions:

1. Preheat the oven to 375°F (190°C).
2. Spray cooking oil into six muffin tins.
3. Blend quinoa, banana, almond butter, and yoghurt in a large bowl.
4. Add blueberries to the mixture.

5. Pour the batter into the prepared muffin tins and bake for 20-25 minutes or until golden brown.

Peanut Butter Banana Breakfast Cookies [9]

Servings: 10 cookies

Ingredients:

- 1 small banana (mashed)
- 6 tablespoons natural peanut butter
- ½ teaspoon ground cinnamon
- 2 tablespoons all-natural almond butter
- Pinch of sea salt

Instructions:

1. Preheat the oven to 350°F (175°C) and line a baking tray with grease-proof paper.
2. Mash the banana in a bowl and stir in peanut butter, cinnamon, and almond butter until well combined.
3. Roll or scoop the batter into 10 balls, place them on the baking tray, and lightly press each cookie with a fork.
4. Bake the cookies for 10 minutes or until the bottoms start to brown.
5. Sprinkle with a pinch of sea salt and enjoy.

Vegan Chocolate Chip Pancakes [10]

Servings: 3

Ingredients:

- ¼ cup vegan chocolate chips
- 1½ teaspoon baking powder
- 1 cup all-purpose flour
- ¾ cup unsweetened plant-based milk
- 1 very ripe banana

Instructions:

1. Mash the banana in a bowl and add the plant-based milk. Whisk them well.
2. Add the baking powder and flour, then whisk until smooth.
3. Spray oil in a flat pan or skillet and set the temperature to medium. Then add a small ladle of pancake batter.
4. Flip and cook the other side when the corners have hardened and the centre is bubbling.
5. Stack the pancakes and top with a few more chocolate chips.

Tofu Scramble with Spinach [11]

Servings: 2

Ingredients:

- 1 cup baby spinach
- ½ tablespoon unsweetened almond milk
- 1 block of firm tofu
- 1½ tablespoons nutritional yeast
- Seasonings: salt, onion powder, garlic powder, ground turmeric, etc.

Instructions:

1. Lightly press the tofu for no more than 20 minutes to drain any extra water.
2. Place the tofu in a medium-sized pan sprayed with cooking spray.
3. Use a spatula to break up the tofu into small bits.
4. Add almond milk, nutritional yeast, and seasonings.
5. Stir well and cook for about 5-7 minutes.

6. Add the spinach and mix until it has just wilted.

Coconut Yoghurt Parfait [12]

Serving: 1

Ingredients:

- ½ cup plain coconut yoghurt
- ¼ cup mixed fresh berries
- 1 tablespoon chopped dried cherries
- 2 chopped dates
- ⅓ cup granola

Instructions:

1. Layer half the yoghurt, half the granola, and all the dates and cherries in a parfait glass.
2. Garnish with the remaining berries, granola, and yoghurt.

Almond Butter Toast with Berries [13]

Serving: 1

Ingredients:

- 1-2 slices toasted bread
- ½ teaspoon chia or hemp seeds
- ¼ cup fresh berries
- 1 tablespoon coconut flakes

- 2 tablespoons almond butter

Instructions:

1. Spread the toast with almond butter.
2. Place the fresh berries on top.
3. Sprinkle with coconut flakes and chia or hemp seeds.

Cinnamon Raisin Oatmeal [14]

Servings: 2

Ingredients:

- 1 cup old-fashioned rolled oats
- ¼ cup vanilla rice or soy milk
- ¼ teaspoon cinnamon
- ¼ cup raisins
- ⅛ teaspoon iodised salt, if available in shops; otherwise, use any salt

Instructions:

1. Boil 2 cups of water in a saucepan with oats, cinnamon, raisins, and salt.
2. Reduce heat and simmer for approximately 10 minutes, stirring regularly, or until cooked to your preference.
3. Serve with vanilla rice or soy milk.

Mango Chia Seed Pudding [15]

Servings: 2

Ingredients:

- 1 cup mango
- 3 tablespoons chia seeds
- 1⅔ cup coconut milk
- 1 teaspoon pure vanilla
- Maple syrup to taste

Instructions:

1. Combine mango, coconut milk, vanilla, and maple syrup in a high-speed blender until creamy and smooth.
2. Add chia seeds and put the mixture in a glass bowl.
3. Leave it in the fridge overnight.

Peanut Butter Banana Smoothie [16]

Servings: 2

Ingredients:

- ¼ cup creamy peanut butter
- 2 ripe bananas
- 3 cups vanilla almond or coconut milk
- 1 tablespoon pure maple syrup
- 3-4 tablespoons cocoa powder

Instructions:

1. Put all the ingredients in a blender and process until smooth.

Blueberry Almond Overnight Oats [17]

Servings: 6

Ingredients:

- 1 cup fresh blueberries
- Pure maple syrup to taste
- 2 cups old-fashioned rolled oats
- 2½ cups unsweetened almond milk
- 2 tablespoons chia seeds

Instructions:

1. Combine the almond milk, oats, chia seeds, and maple syrup in a large bowl. Stir well.
2. Cover with plastic wrap and keep in the refrigerator overnight.
3. You can add blueberries before placing your oats in the fridge or in the morning for a burst of freshness.

Vegan Breakfast Burrito [18]

Servings: 6

Ingredients:

- 6 burrito-sized tortillas
- 1½ cups dairy-free cheese, grated
- 3 cups refried beans home-made or bought in-store (black or pinto beans as an alternative)
- 1 teaspoon paprika
- 1 teaspoon garlic powder

Instructions:

1. Spread ½ cup of beans on each tortilla.
2. Top with seasonings and add ½ cup of cheese on top.
3. Fold the sides down for 5 minutes until it's sealed and brown.
4. Flip it to the other side and cook for another 5 minutes.

Chocolate Banana Protein Shake [19]

Serving: 1

Ingredients:

- ½ ripe banana
- 1½ tablespoons cocoa powder
- 1 scoop (25g) of your favourite plant-based protein powder (pea protein, soy protein, or a blend of plant proteins)
- 1 tablespoon maple syrup
- ½ cup unsweetened almond milk

Instructions:

1. Blend all the ingredients on high speed until smooth.
2. Add almond milk and blend again if the shake is too thick.

Quick and Nutrient-Packed Lunches

These nutritious vegan lunches are tailored to your busy schedule. They're delicious and super easy to prepare. You'll be amazed by how satisfying and healthy your midday meal can be. These recipes are designed to keep you fuelled and focused throughout your day of classes and studying. So, let's dive into these tasty options and make your lunch break something to look forward to.

Most of these lunch recipes can be portioned and stored in the fridge or freezer, making them convenient for quick, future meals.

Simple Buddha Bowl [20]

Servings: 2

Ingredients:

- ¼ cup kimchee or sauerkraut
- ½ cup sliced radish
- ½ cup edamame beans
- ½ cup kale
- 2 cups cooked farro

Instructions:

1. Combine all ingredients in a bowl.
2. You can add your favourite salad dressing or seasoning for extra flavour.

Tips:

- You can prepare all the ingredients in advance and combine them when you are ready to eat.
- Instead of farro, you can use other grains like rice, quinoa, or couscous.
- You can make a couple of Buddha bowls and keep them in the fridge for a day or two.

Simple Buddha Bowl combos can be made of:

- Greens and vegetables like spinach, kale, broccoli, mushrooms, carrots, bell peppers, etc.
- Starches like buckwheat, quinoa, brown rice, whole grain bread, whole grain pasta, sweet potatoes, etc.
- Any legumes: lentils, beans, tempeh, tofu, etc.
- Condiments like nuts or seeds, seasonings, sauces, dressings, herbs, etc.

Mediterranean Chickpea Salad [21]

Serving: 1

Ingredients:

- ½ cup cooked brown rice
- ⅓ cup diced tomatoes
- ½ cup diced cucumbers
- ½ cup chickpeas
- 2 cups chopped spinach

Instructions:

1. Combine all the ingredients in a salad bowl.
2. Add hummus, lemon juice, or parsley to taste.

Tips:

- Prep the ingredients in larger quantities to make multiple servings.
- This salad is versatile. Customise it with your favourite vegetables and seasonings.

Quinoa Salad with Veggies [22]

Servings: 2-3

Ingredients:

- 1 cup quinoa
- 2 cups low-sodium vegetable broth
- ¼-½ avocado
- 2-3 handfuls spring mix lettuce
- ⅓-½ cup carrots, shredded or sliced

Instructions:

1. Put the quinoa and vegetable broth in a saucepan and boil, then lower the heat, cover, and simmer for 15-20 minutes or until the quinoa is cooked.
2. Add sliced or chopped carrots and avocado once quinoa is done.
3. Serve over spring mix lettuce and season with a bit of pepper and lemon juice.

- Cook a large portion of quinoa and store it in the fridge or freezer for the future.
- You can use your favourite vegetables and dressings with this salad.

Hummus and Veggie Wrap [23]

Servings: 4

Ingredients:

- 4 large tortillas
- 2 julienned carrots
- 2 bell peppers
- ½ cup cooked mushrooms
- 1 cup hummus

Instructions:

1. Place the tortilla on a cutting board and spread it with hummus.
2. Top with vegetables, wrap up and cut in half.

Tips:

- You can make wraps in the morning and pack them for lunch.
- For extra nutrition, you can add greens like spinach or kale.

Simple Chickpea Salad [24]

Servings: 2

Ingredients:

- 1½ cups chickpeas, drained and rinsed
- ⅓ cup pickles, finely chopped
- ⅓ cup celery stalk, finely chopped
- ¼ cup red onions, finely chopped
- 2 tablespoons vegan mayonnaise

Instructions:

1. Use a potato masher to mash all the ingredients in a medium bowl thoroughly. It's okay to have a few whole chickpeas left over.
2. Combine the vegan mayonnaise with the chopped celery, red onions, and pickles, and mix thoroughly.
3. Add your favourite seasoning.

Mediterranean Rice Bowl [25]

Servings: 2

Ingredients:

- ½ cup brown rice, cooked
- 10 black or green olives, pitted
- 10 cherry tomatoes
- 1 cup vegan feta cheese
- Tahini sauce

Instructions:

1. Place the cooked brown rice in the bowl.
2. Top with crumbled vegan feta cheese, olives, cherry tomatoes, and tahini sauce.
3. Add spinach, cucumber, arugula, or hummus if you like.

Black Bean and Corn Salad [26]

Servings: 4

Ingredients:

- 1½ cups corn, drained and rinsed
- 1½ cups black beans, drained and rinsed
- 1 teaspoon olive oil
- 1 cup fresh salsa, homemade or purchased
- ¼ teaspoon cumin

Instructions:

1. Mix all ingredients in a bowl and enjoy a quick and easy salad.
2. Add any seasoning you like.

Chickpea Salad Wrap [27]

Servings: 4

Ingredients:

- 1 cup chickpeas, drained and rinsed

- 2 large carrots, sliced
- 1 red pepper, sliced
- 1 cup spinach
- 4 10" flour tortilla shells

Instructions:

1. Spread each ingredient equally across the four wraps.
2. Fold up the wraps and enjoy.

Avocado and Tomato Sandwich [28]

Serving: 1

Ingredients:

- 1 slice ciabatta bread
- ½ avocado, mashed
- 3 tomato slices
- 1 teaspoon garlic salt
- 1 pinch ground black pepper

Instructions:

1. In a small bowl, combine avocado and garlic salt.
2. Spread this mixture onto ciabatta bread, top with tomatoes, and season with black pepper.

Quinoa and Black Bean Bowl [29]

Servings: 4

Ingredients:

- 3 cups cooked white quinoa
- 1½ cups black beans
- 1 cup corn kernels, fresh or frozen
- 1 cup jarred salsa
- 1 tablespoon ground cumin

Instructions:

1. Preheat a large saucepan over medium heat.
2. Add corn and black beans and cook for 3 minutes, stirring occasionally.
3. Add cumin and quinoa and cook for another 3 minutes.
4. Add jarred salsa and cook for about 2 minutes until quinoa starts drying out.

Vegan Caesar Salad [30]

Servings: 4

Ingredients:

- 1-1½ cups croutons
- 6 cups romaine, chopped
- ⅓-½ cup vegan Caesar dressing
- ½ cup shaved vegan parmesan
- Fresh pepper

Instructions:

1. Combine all the ingredients in a bowl and serve right away.

Thai Peanut Noodle Salad [31]

Servings: 4

Ingredients:

- 6 cups water
- 4 cups thin spaghetti
- 3 tablespoons peanut butter
- 3 tablespoons light soy sauce
- ¾ teaspoon sriracha sauce

Instructions:

1. Cook the noodles for 5-7 minutes on high heat.
2. Add the sriracha, peanut butter, and soy sauce. Mix thoroughly.
3. You can add green onions or peanuts for more taste.

Vegan Sushi Bowl [32]

Servings: 4

Ingredients:

- 1 package tofu
- 1 avocado, diced
- 1 cup sushi rice

- 2 sheets of nori
- 2-4 tablespoons soy sauce

Instructions:

1. Start by baking tofu for 20 minutes at 350°F (175°C).
2. Make sushi rice following the instructions on the package.
3. Separate the rice into four bowls.
4. Distribute the tofu among the bowls, top with chunks of avocado and a quarter of the nori strips.
5. Sprinkle with a little soy sauce to taste.

Mediterranean Couscous Salad [33]

Servings: 4

Ingredients:

- 2¾ cups couscous, cooked (whole wheat couscous is the best, if available)
- 2 cups spinach
- 5-6 cherry tomatoes, chopped
- ½ cauliflower
- 1 garlic clove, chopped

Instructions:

1. Wash the cauliflower and cut it into small pieces, then bake for 20-25 minutes in a preheated oven at 450°F (230°C).
2. Season with pepper, salt, and olive oil for extra taste.
3. In a large bowl, combine all the ingredients and serve.
4. Feel free to drizzle a parsley pesto dressing, made from lemon juice, olive oil, and parsley on your salad.

Tips:

1. This salad is versatile. You can swap any ingredients from this list: swap couscous with quinoa or brown rice, swap cauliflower with broccoli, carrots, or squash, swap spinach with Swiss chard.
2. You can store this salad in the fridge for 3-4 days. It's not recommended to freeze it as couscous can become mushy after it's been defrosted.

Spinach and Strawberry Salad [34]

Servings: 4

Ingredients:

- ¾ cup fresh strawberries
- ¼ cup red onions, sliced
- 7½ cups fresh baby spinach
- Balsamic vinaigrette
- ¼ cup chopped pecans

Instructions:

1. Mix all the ingredients in a bowl.
2. Dress the salad with balsamic vinaigrette, or make your dressing using balsamic vinegar and olive oil.

Vegan Caprese Salad [35]

Servings: 6

Ingredients:

- 1 block super-firm tofu
- 4 cups tomatoes
- 12-14 large basil leaves
- 1 lemon
- Salt

Instructions:

1. Begin with dicing tofu into ½-inch cubes or slices.

2. Marinate your tofu slices in lemon juice and salt for at least 4 hours, or leave overnight in the fridge.
3. Slice or dice tomatoes and serve your salad with basil leaves.

Vegan Lentil Soup [36]

Servings: 4

Ingredients:

- 1 cup brown lentils
- 1 large onion, chopped

- ½ cup sliced baby carrots
- 3 sweet potatoes, diced
- 3 tablespoons Better than Bouillon

Instructions:

1. Place sweet potatoes and baby carrots in a large saucepan filled with water and cook on high heat.
2. Meanwhile, sauté onion in a frying pan. When golden brown, add onions and lentils to the saucepan.
3. When water boils, add 3 spoons of Better than Bouillon.
4. Lower the heat, stir, and simmer for 30-40 minutes or until lentils and potatoes are tender.

Tips:

1. Better than Bouillon is a healthier and tastier option than traditional bouillon, but also more expensive. If you're on a very tight budget, it's okay to use vegan bouillon as an alternative to help you manage your expenses.
2. Portion it and store it in the fridge or freezer.

Roasted Red Pepper Hummus Wrap [37]

Servings: 4

Ingredients:

- 4 wraps
- 2 cups roasted red peppers, sliced
- 3 ¾ cups baby spinach leaves

- ½ cup hummus
- 1 cucumber, sliced

Instructions:

1. Spread hummus over each wrap.
2. Top with cucumber, red pepper, and spinach leaves.
3. Add salt and pepper to taste if desired.
4. Roll up.
5. Cut in half and serve.

Sweet Potato and Black Bean Quesadilla [38]

Servings: 6

Ingredients:

- 1 large sweet potato, steamed or baked
- 6 corn tortillas
- ¾ cup black beans, cooked
- ½ cup vegan mozzarella, shredded
- ½ teaspoon garlic powder

Instructions:

1. In a mixing bowl, combine mashed sweet potato, garlic powder, cooked black beans and salt (optional).
2. Preheat a frying pan to medium heat, remove a tortilla from the bag, and cook each side for 30-40 seconds.
3. Fill one half of the tortilla with the sweet potato and black bean mixture and add some grated vegan cheese.

4. Make a half-moon shape by folding the other side over and cook on both sides until crispy and the cheese is melted.
5. Repeat the process with each tortilla until you finish all the mixture.

Tips:

1. Feel free to adjust the quantity of the ingredients to your liking.

Simple Dinners for Busy Evenings

These vegan dinner options are student-friendly, easy to prepare, and packed with flavours and nutrients. Most of these meals are ideal for batch cooking. Once cooked, portion them and store them in the freezer to have ready meals whenever needed.

They are ideal for meeting the demands of student life. They won't break the bank or take too much of your valuable study time to prepare.

Pasta with Pesto and Cherry Tomatoes [39]

Servings: 3-4

Ingredients:

- ½ cup homemade vegan cashew pesto

- 1 cup bucatini pasta
- 1 cup cherry tomatoes, sliced
- 2 tablespoons olive oil
- ¼-½ teaspoon kosher salt (if using table salt, use approximately half as much)

Instructions:

1. Cook pasta. Then drain, leaving in reserve ¼ cup of the pasta water.
2. Add the reserved pasta water, sliced cherry tomatoes, pesto, salt, and olive oil. Stir well and serve.

One-Pot Rice and Lentils [40]

Servings: 4-6

Ingredients:

- 1 cup dried lentils
- 1 cup brown basmati rice
- 1 large onion, chopped
- 4 cups low-sodium vegetable broth (if not available, you can use low-salt vegetable stock cubes and 4 cups of water)
- 1 tablespoon garlic powder

Instructions:

1. In a medium saucepan, sauté the onion for 2-3 minutes and add the broth, rice, and lentils.

2. Bring it to a boil, lower heat, and simmer for approximately 45 minutes, or until rice and lentils are tender.
3. Leave it to cool for another 10 minutes after cooking.
4. Eat it alone or serve with your favourite fresh vegetables.

Teriyaki Tofu Stir-Fry [41]

Servings: 4-6

Ingredients:

- 2 cups Asian-style vegetable stir fry mix
- 1 block extra firm tofu, diced
- 2 teaspoons olive oil
- Organic jasmine rice, microwave packet
- 2 cups Soyaki sauce

Instructions:

1. Add olive oil and tofu to a large saucepan and cook for 7-10 minutes or until the tofu is browned on all sides.
2. Add ½-1 cup Soyaki sauce and the vegetables mix to the saucepan.
3. Cover and cook, stirring occasionally, for 10-12 minutes or until vegetables are softened.
4. Prepare the rice in the microwave according to the packaging, then put about ½-¾ cup of rice in the bowl or on the serving plate.
5. Top with a generous serving of the tofu and vegetable stir-fry mixture.
6. Garnish with sliced green onions if desired.

Courgette Noodles with Tomato Sauce [42]

Servings: 2

Ingredients:

- 1 medium courgette, spiralised
- 1 small red onion, diced
- 1 garlic clove, crushed
- 2 cups passata
- ½ cup canned chickpeas, drained

Instructions:

1. In a non-stick pan, sauté onion and garlic for 1-2 minutes, then add passata and chickpeas.
2. Cover and cook on low heat for about 5 minutes.

3. Add the courgette and cook for a minute, tossing continuously.
4. Season to taste.

Vegan Black Bean Burger [43]

Servings: 3

Ingredients:

- 2 cups cooked black beans
- 1 medium courgette, shredded
- 3 tablespoons ground flaxseed
- 1 tablespoon chilli powder
- ½ teaspoon salt

Instructions:

1. Mash half of the black beans, then add courgette and spices.
2. Stir well to combine all the ingredients.
3. Form the burgers into six burger patties.
4. Cook the patties in a non-stick frying pan over medium heat for up to 6 minutes on each side.
5. Enjoy with your favourite toppings.
6. Serve with salad.

Vegan Broccoli Alfredo [44]

Servings: 1-2

Ingredients:

- ½ head of chopped broccoli or ½ bag of a frozen one
- 1½-2 cups of dry pasta (choose your favourite)
- 2 garlic cloves, smashed
- Olive oil
- Salt
- 1 tablespoon hemp hearts (optional)

Instructions:

1. Bring a large pot of water to the boil. Add a generous sprinkle of salt to the pot for extra taste.
2. In a non-stick pan, fry the broccoli and smashed garlic in olive oil. Add some salt and cook until the broccoli is bright green and tender.

3. Cook the pasta and reserve about half the cup of pasta water after draining.
4. Blend the reserved pasta water, hemp hearts if you're using, cooked broccoli and garlic with 1-2 spoons of cooked pasta until you reach the desired texture.
5. Toss the mixture with the rest of the pasta and serve.

One-Pot Lentil Stew [45]

Servings: 4

Ingredients:

- 1⅓ cups lentils
- 1 large onion, finely diced
- 3 tablespoons vegetable oil
- ¼ cup tomato paste
- Salt or/and curry powder to taste

Instructions:

1. In a saucepan, sauté the onion until almost brown.
2. Stir in the lentils for 1 minute, then add the tomato paste and seasonings.
3. Stir well to mix the ingredients evenly.
4. Add water and cook for about 20 minutes or until the lentils are tender.

Tips:

1. You can store this in an airtight container in the freezer or the fridge for up to 5 days.

Vegan Butternut Squash Soup [46]

Servings: 2

Ingredients:

- 1¾ butternut squash
- 2½ cloves garlic
- 8 tablespoons dairy-free Greek yoghurt
- 1 red onion
- Salt and pepper to taste

Instructions:

1. Preheat the oven to 425°F (215°C).
2. Slice butternut squash in half lengthwise, sprinkle with a bit of water, season with salt, and bake for about 20 minutes until cooked.
3. Add unpeeled garlic cloves and red onion wedges to the baking dish.
4. Season with salt and drizzle with olive oil. Roast for an additional 20 minutes.
5. Place all the ingredients in the blender, including dairy-free Greek yoghurt. Squeeze the roasted garlic cloves from their skins and blend everything until smooth.
6. Serve by adding another spoonful of Greek yoghurt and season with black pepper (optional).

Spaghetti Aglio E Olio [47]

Servings: 4

Ingredients:

- 200g or 2 cups spaghetti or your favourite pasta
- 3 medium-sized fresh chillies, deseeded and chopped (you can substitute them with dried chillies)
- 3 tablespoons olive oil
- 6 cloves minced garlic
- Salt and pepper to season

Instructions:

1. Cook spaghetti according to package instructions.
2. Drain and leave half a cup of pasta water to use later.
3. Combine minced garlic and olive oil in the saucepan or the frying pan, and sauté for a minute on low heat, then add spaghetti and mix well.
4. Add chopped chillies and sauté for another 2 minutes.
5. Add cooked pasta and toss well for a minute at medium heat.
6. Add reserved pasta water with a bit of salt and toss until combined.
7. To serve, add pepper and chopped parsley if you wish, and mix well.

BBQ-Baked Tofu [48]

Servings: 4

Ingredients:

- 1 block super-firm tofu
- ⅓ cup BBQ sauce
- 1 tablespoon neutral oil, canola, or any vegetable
- 1 tablespoon reduced-sodium soy sauce
- 1 tablespoon Sambal Oelek (if you don't have it, the best substitutes are garlic and chilli sauce or crushed chilli)

Instructions:

1. Set the oven to 420°F (215°C).
2. Remove liquid from the tofu, pat dry with a paper towel, and cut into squares or triangles.
3. Mix tofu with soy sauce, Sambal Oelek, and oil in a bowl, then bake for 15-20 minutes or until golden.
4. Add baked tofu to the bowl and cover with BBQ sauce.
5. Bake for 10-20 minutes until tofu is almost blackened.

Vegan Stuffed Bell Pepper [49]

Servings: 4

Ingredients:

- 1½ cups mixed beans
- 2 cups cauliflower rice
- 4 bell peppers, halved

- 1 cup marinara sauce
- ½ cup vegan cheese, shredded

Instructions:

1. Preheat the oven to 350°F (175°C).
2. Cook cauliflower rice in the microwave for 2 minutes.
3. Mix marinara sauce, vegan cheese, and mixed beans in the bowl, and season with salt and pepper if you like.
4. Stuff the halved bell peppers with the mixture and top with vegan cheese.
5. Bake the peppers in the oven for 20-30 minutes and serve with marinara sauce.
6. Seve with roasted sweet potatoes and/or salad of your choice.

One-Pot Curry Lentils [50]

Servings: 4

Ingredients:

- 1 can tinned tomatoes
- 1 can lentils
- 1 small onion, coarsely grated
- 2 tablespoons curry powder
- 4 tablespoons coconut milk

Instructions:

1. In a large saucepan, sauté onion until light brown.
2. Add canned tomatoes and curry powder and stir.
3. Cook for 5-6 minutes over medium-low heat, stirring periodically.
4. Add lentils and cook for another 1-2 minutes.
5. Stir in the coconut milk.
6. Once it begins to simmer, remove from the heat.
7. Season with salt and pepper if you wish.
8. You can eat it on its own or serve it with rice and fresh vegetables.

Roasted Vegetable Quinoa Bowl [51]

Servings: 6

Ingredients:

- 1 batch of roasted vegetables
- 6 cups quinoa, cooked
- 1 batch of crispy roasted chickpeas

- 1 batch of hemp seed pesto
- Green onions, chopped.

Instructions:

1. Cook quinoa according to the instructions on the packaging.
2. Roast vegetables and chickpeas.
3. Place cooked quinoa in a bowl.
4. Top it with roasted chickpeas and roasted veggies.
5. Drizzle with hemp seed pesto and garnish with chopped green onions.

Vegan Stir-Fried Rice [52]

Servings: 3

Ingredients:

- 3 cups rice, cooked
- 2 scallions
- 1 large carrot, chopped
- 1 cup frozen peas
- 3 tablespoons soy sauce

Instructions:

1. Sauté carrot for 2 minutes in a non-stick pan.
2. Add the cooked rice and cook while stirring until the rice is slightly brown.
3. Stir in the frozen peas and cook for another 3-5 minutes.
4. Add soy sauce and scallions, mix well, and serve.

Vegan Sweet Potato Curry [53]

Servings: 3

Ingredients:

- 1 sweet potato, peeled and chopped
- 1 large yellow onion, chopped
- 1½ cups coconut milk
- 1½ cups chickpeas, drained and rinsed
- 4 tablespoons curry paste

Instructions:

1. In a large saucepan, sauté onion for 5-6 minutes. You can use avocado oil or coconut oil if you like.
2. Add curry paste and cook for a minute.
3. Stir in coconut milk, chickpeas, and sweet potatoes.
4. Bring to the boil, reduce the heat and simmer for 10-15 minutes.
5. If needed, season with salt and pepper.

Mushroom and Spinach Risotto [(54)]

Servings: 4

Ingredients:

- 1½ cups mushrooms
- 8¼ cups spinach
- 1 small onion
- 3⅓ cups vegetable broth
- 1 cup risotto rice

Instructions:

1. In a pot, cook onion until slightly brown.
2. Stir in the mushrooms and cook until soft.
3. Add the risotto rice and cook for 2 minutes, stirring occasionally.

4. Add the broth and chopped spinach.
5. If needed, season with salt and pepper.

Courgette Noodles with Pesto [55]

Servings: 4

Ingredients:

- 1 batch of vegan pesto
- 1 large courgette, spiralised
- 12 cherry tomatoes, halved
- 1 tablespoon coconut or olive oil
- 1 tablespoon fresh basil, thinly sliced

Instructions:

1. Add the oil to a frying pan and stir in the noodles.
2. Cook for 3-4 minutes.
3. Serve your courgette noodles with pesto and cherry tomatoes.
4. Garnish with fresh basil.

Cauliflower Buffalo Wings [56]

Servings: 4

Ingredients:

- 1 cauliflower, cut into 1-inch chunks
- 1 cup buffalo sauce
- ¾ cup unsweetened non-dairy milk

- ¾ cup flour
- ½ teaspoon each: onion powder, garlic powder, paprika

Instructions:

1. Set the oven to 450°F (230°C).
2. Combine flour, milk, and seasonings in a bowl to make the dipping batter.
3. Dip cauliflower chunks in the batter to thoroughly coat each and place them on a baking sheet.
4. Bake for about 20 minutes, flipping halfway.
5. Remove the tray from the oven. Dip each chunk in buffalo sauce and grill for 6-10 minutes.
6. Serve with grilled vegetables.

Vegan Chilli [57]

Serving: 1

Ingredients:

- 3 medium sweet potatoes, peeled and chopped
- 1 medium onion, diced
- 2 cups vegetable broth
- 1½ cup black beans
- 2 cups jar salsa

Instructions:

1. Start by cooking the onion in a saucepan over medium heat until slightly brown.
2. Add in sweet potatoes and cook for 3 minutes.
3. Stir in vegetable broth, salsa, and any seasoning you choose.
4. Bring to the boil, reduce the heat, add beans, and simmer for 20-30 minutes.
5. Serve with spring onion if desired.

Teriyaki Portobello Mushrooms [58]

Servings: 2

Ingredients:

- 3-4 portobello mushrooms, sliced ½ inch
- 2 tablespoons teriyaki marinade
- 1 clove garlic, thinly sliced
- 2 tablespoons vegan butter
- 2 tablespoons olive oil

Instructions:

1. Heat butter and oil in a frying pan and stir in mushrooms, teriyaki marinade, and garlic.
2. Cook for 5 minutes or until mushrooms are slightly brown.
3. Reduce the heat and simmer for 5-8 minutes.
4. These teriyaki portobello mushrooms taste delicious with rice.

Snacks and Sides

Guacamole and Veggie Sticks [59]

Serving: 1

Ingredients:

- 1 avocado, halved
- ¼ cup plum tomatoes, diced
- 1 lime, juiced
- 1 garlic clove, minced
- 2 tablespoons chopped coriander

Instructions:

1. In a bowl, mash the avocado and lime juice.
2. Add the garlic, coriander, and tomatoes, folding into the avocado mixture.

3. Season with salt and pepper, if needed.
4. Serve with your favourite vegetable sticks like cucumbers, carrots, celery, or baked sweet potato wedges.

Vegan Courgette Fritters [60]

Servings: 6 fritters

Ingredients:

- 4 small courgettes, grated
- 1 yellow onion, thinly sliced
- ½ cup all-purpose or chickpea flour
- 1 garlic clove, thinly sliced
- ½ teaspoon baking powder

Instructions:

1. Place grated courgettes in a bowl, add salt, and let it sit for half an hour.
2. In another bowl, combine baking powder and flour. Sprinkle with a little bit of salt if you like.
3. Remove the liquid from the courgette and place it in a bowl with the flour mixture.
4. Mix well and form fritters.
5. Fry them in a frying pan on medium heat until both sides are golden.

Vegan Cinnamon Roasted Chickpeas ⁽⁶¹⁾

Servings: 1

Ingredients:

- 1¾ cups chickpeas
- 2½ teaspoons ground cinnamon
- 2 teaspoons coconut sugar
- ½ tablespoon coconut oil
- 2 tablespoons maple syrup

Instructions:

1. Preheat the oven to 350°F (175°C).
2. Gently rub the chickpeas between two towels to remove the skins.
3. Line a baking tray with baking paper and place the chickpeas on the tray.
4. In a bowl, combine chickpeas, coconut oil, and maple syrup, then place them on the baking tray and bake for 40-45 minutes, tossing the chickpeas every 10-15 minutes.
5. Sprinkle 2½ teaspoons ground cinnamon on top and coconut sugar at the end.

Vegan Spinach Dip [62]

Servings: 12

Ingredients:

- 10 cups spinach
- ¼ teaspoon paprika
- ½ cup vegan mayonnaise
- 2 tablespoons vegan sour cream
- 1 packet of onion soup mix

Instructions:

1. In a large bowl, mix all the ingredients and keep covered for 15 minutes or overnight.

Cucumber and Carrot Slaw [63]

Servings: 2

Ingredients:

- 2 medium carrots
- 1 large English cucumber
- 2 tablespoons rice vinegar or 1 tablespoon cider vinegar
- ½ teaspoon sesame oil
- ½ teaspoon sugar

Instructions:

1. Cut the cucumber and carrots into long strips using a julienne peeler or grater.
2. In a medium bowl, combine all the ingredients.
3. You can also add a teaspoon of water to reduce the taste of vinegar.
4. Garnish with coriander and/or sesame seeds before serving.

Vegan Cheesy Popcorn [64]

Servings: 2

Ingredients:

- ⅓ cup popcorn kernels
- 2 teaspoons nutritional yeast flakes
- Vegetable spray
- ¼ teaspoon turmeric

- ½ teaspoon paprika

Instructions:

1. Spray the oil in a pan, place it on the hob on a medium heat, and add two popcorn kernels.
2. Once the kernels pop, remove them and add in the remaining kernels.
3. Put the pan back on the hob and tilt the lid slightly to allow steam to escape. Keep shaking the pan until you can't hear any more popping.
4. Add the nutritional yeast, paprika, turmeric, or any seasoning you choose.

Baked Sweet Potato Fries [65]

Servings: 4

Ingredients:

- 3 large sweet potatoes
- ¼ teaspoon paprika
- 1 teaspoon cumin
- 1 tablespoon extra virgin olive oil
- ½ teaspoon kosher salt

Instructions:

1. Preheat the oven to 400°F (200°C).
2. Peel and cut sweet potatoes into sticks or wedges.
3. Combine all the ingredients in a bowl so that the sweet potatoes are fully coated with spices and oil.

4. Line a baking tray with baking paper and place the potatoes on the paper in a single layer.
5. Bake for about 30 minutes, tossing halfway to ensure the fries bake evenly.

Vegan Mango Salsa [66]

Servings: 6

Ingredients:

- 1½ mangoes, diced
- 2 large Roma tomatoes, diced
- 2 Serrano chiles, minced
- ½ red onion, diced
- 3 tablespoons coriander, minced

Instructions:

1. In a large mixing bowl, combine all the ingredients and serve with your favourite tacos.
2. You can also add lime juice or any seasoning you choose.

Garlic Hummus [67]

Serving: 1

Ingredients:

- 1½ cups chickpeas, drained and rinsed
- 4 tablespoons extra virgin olive oil

- 2 garlic heads
- 2 tablespoons tahini
- 1 lemon, juiced

Instructions:

1. Set the oven to 350°F (175°C).
2. Cut the tips off every garlic clove and place root-side down in a small baking dish or on a sheet of aluminium foil.
3. Top the cut ends of the garlic with 2 tablespoons extra virgin olive oil, and cover with foil before roasting for about 30 minutes.
4. Remove the garlic skin and place the cloves in a food processor.
5. Add the remaining ingredients and blend for about a minute. You can add any spices you like.
6. Keep in an airtight container for up to 5 days.

Edamame with Sea Salt (68)

Serving: 1

Ingredients:

- 1 cup frozen edamame beans
- 2 tablespoons salt
- 4¼ cups water
- Flaky sea salt for serving
- Sesame oil for serving

Instructions:

1. Bring a large saucepan of water to a boil and add salt to it.
2. Once salt is dissolved, add edamame beans and cook for about 5 minutes over medium heat.
3. Drain the edamame and rinse with cold water.
4. Serve with sesame oil, flaky sea salt and/or sesame seeds.

Sliced Apples with Almond Butter [69]

Servings: 1

Ingredients:

- ¼ cup almond butter
- 1 apple
- ¼ cup dark chocolate chips
- 2 tablespoons walnuts
- 2 tablespoons sliced almonds

Instructions:

1. Cross-cut the apple.
2. Sprinkle the almonds, walnuts, and dark chocolate chips on top of each slice after spreading it with almond butter.

Homemade Hummus and Veggie Dippers [70]

Servings: 6

Ingredients:

- 1¾ cups chickpeas
- 3 tablespoons lemon juice
- ⅓ cup tahini
- 2 tablespoons olive oil
- 1 garlic clove

Instructions:

1. Rinse the chickpeas and place them in the food processor.
2. Add garlic, olive oil, tahini, lemon juice, optional salt, pepper, or cumin, and blend until creamy.
3. Serve with assorted veggies.

Crispy Baked Tofu Fingers [71]

Servings: 4

Ingredients:

- 1 block extra firm tofu
- ½ cup whole wheat breadcrumbs
- ⅓ cup tamari or soy sauce
- ¼ teaspoon salt
- 1 tablespoon Italian seasoning

Instructions:

1. Set the oven to 425°F (215°C).
2. Wrap the tofu with a paper towel and place on a plate. Put another plate on top and place something heavy on it. Let it sit for about 20 minutes.
3. Slice the tofu and put it in a bowl with tamari or soy sauce. Let it sit for 10 minutes.
4. In a separate bowl, combine breadcrumbs and seasonings. Add in marinated tofu fingers.
5. Bake the tofu for 20 minutes on a non-stick baking sheet. Flip and cook for an additional 5 minutes.

Cucumber Slices with Hummus [72]

Servings: 2

Ingredients:

- ½ cup hummus
- 1 cucumber, sliced in about ¼ inch thick

- 2 or 3 kalamata olives, sliced
- 4 or 5 cherry tomatoes, cut in half
- Everything Bagel Seasoning

Instructions:

1. Top each cucumber slice with a spoon of hummus, sprinkle with the seasoning and top with a slice of tomato and/or olive.

Vegan Spicy Roasted Almonds [73]

Servings: 4

Ingredients:

- 1 cup raw almonds
- 2 teaspoons extra virgin olive oil
- 1 teaspoon cayenne pepper
- 1 teaspoon sea salt flakes
- ½ teaspoon garlic powder

Instructions:

1. Preheat the oven to 350°F (175°C).
2. Use baking paper to line a baking sheet.
3. In a bowl, combine all the ingredients.
4. Place the almonds on the baking tray.
5. Roast for 7 minutes, turn the almonds, and then roast for 7-8 minutes.

Crispy Roasted Chickpeas [74]

Servings: 4

Ingredients:

- 1 can chickpeas, drained and rinsed
- ¼ teaspoon dried thyme
- 2 teaspoons extra virgin olive oil
- ½ teaspoon orange zest
- ⅛ teaspoon sea or kosher salt

Instructions:

1. Set the oven to 450°F (230°C).
2. Spread the chickpeas on a fresh kitchen towel and gently wipe them to remove moisture.
3. Spread the chickpeas on a baking sheet and top with the oil.
4. Sprinkle with salt, orange zest and thyme. Mix well and bake for about 10 minutes.
5. Shake the tray and bake for another 10 minutes until the chickpeas are crispy.

Vegan Spring Rolls [75]

Servings: 10 spring rolls

Ingredients:

- 1 small cucumber, thinly sliced
- 10 spring roll wrappers (you can buy a pack of 30)
- 1 carrot, shredded

- ½ a lime
- Sesame oil

Instructions:

1. Dip one spring roll wrapped into the bowl of water for 10 seconds.
2. Shake and place on the cutting board.
3. Drizzle sesame oil on the wrapper, add carrots and cucumbers, and again drizzle with the juice of a lime.
4. You can add any other seasonings of your choice.
5. Wrap each vegan spring roll and serve.
6. You can store it in the fridge for 2-3 days.

Guilt-Free Sweet Potato Fries [76]

Servings: 4

Ingredients:

- 4 medium sweet potatoes, peeled and cut lengthwise into thick slices
- 2 teaspoons cumin powder
- 1 teaspoon chilli powder
- 1 teaspoon garlic powder
- 2 teaspoons salt

Instructions:

1. Preheat the oven to 400°F (200°C).
2. In a large bowl, combine spices and add sweet potato slices. Toss to coat the slices evenly.

3. Place the fries in a single layer on a baking tray lined with greaseproof baking paper.
4. Bake for 20 minutes.
5. Flip the fries and bake for 10 more minutes until crispy.

Guacamole and Salsa for Tortilla Chips [77]

Servings: 5

Ingredients:

- 1 cup cherry tomatoes, diced
- ½ red onion, finely chopped
- 2 large ripe avocados, pitted and diced
- 1 teaspoon Kosher salt
- 2 tablespoons lime juice

Instructions:

1. In a medium bowl, combine all ingredients and season with salt or any seasoning you prefer.
2. Enjoy with tortilla chips.

Baked Falafel Bites [78]

Servings: 4

Ingredients:

- 1 can chickpeas, drained and rinsed
- ½ cup diced red onion
- 1 cup chickpea flour
- 3 cloves garlic, minced
- Seasonings of your choice: parsley, salt, cumin, pepper, coriander, etc.

Instructions:

1. Set the oven to 400°F (200°C).
2. Combine all the ingredients in a food processor, and mix until it looks like chunky sand.
3. Scoop the dough and form the balls.
4. Place the balls on a baking tray lined with greaseproof paper.
5. Bake for 45 minutes. Flip halfway through.

Vegan Spinach Artichoke Dip *(79)*

Servings: 8

Ingredients:

- 3 cups spinach, chopped
- ¼ cup nutritional yeast
- 1 cup egg-free mayo
- 1 can artichoke hearts, chopped
- 4 cloves garlic, minced

Instructions:

1. Set the oven to 350°F (175°C).
2. In an oven-safe baking dish, combine all ingredients and bake for 20 minutes.

Asian Sesame Cucumber Salad [80]

Servings: 2

Ingredients:

- ½ large cucumber, thinly sliced
- 1 teaspoon soy sauce
- 1 tablespoon sesame oil
- 2 tablespoons rice vinegar
- 1 teaspoon sriracha sauce

Instructions:

1. In a small bowl, combine sriracha sauce, rice vinegar, sesame oil, and soy sauce to make the dressing.
2. Pour the dressing over the cucumber slices and stir well.
3. You can top your salad with sesame seeds.

Caprese Skewers [81]

Servings: 4

Ingredients:

- 1 block extra firm tofu
- ½ bunch fresh basil
- 1⅓ cup cherry tomatoes, sliced in half
- 1 teaspoon oregano
- Salt and pepper to tasting

Instructions:

1. Wrap the tofu in a kitchen towel and squeeze the liquid out.
2. Then, slice it into small cubes and mix with oregano, salt, and pepper.
3. Assemble caprese skewers with one cube of tofu, basil leaf, and tomato.

Vegan Mini Quiches [82]

Servings: 8

Ingredients:

- ½ cup chickpea flour
- 8 sundried tomatoes, chopped
- 3 tablespoons nutritional yeast
- ½ medium onion, diced
- 2 garlic cloves, minced

Instructions:

1. Set the oven to 430°F (220°C).
2. Combine sundried tomatoes, nutritional yeast, and chickpea flour in a bowl. Pour about ¾ of a cup of water into the bowl. You can also add salt and seasonings of your choice.
3. Fry the garlic and onion for a few minutes in a frying pan. Let them cool and add to the bowl.

4. Pour the mixture into the muffin tin. You can use some cooking spray. Bake quiches until browned on top, roughly 15-20 minutes.

Vegan Spinach Dip Stuffed Bread [83]

Serving: 1

Ingredients:

- 1 loaf pumpernickel
- 1 cup frozen spinach, thawed
- 1 can artichoke, chopped
- 1 cup vegan cheese, grated
- 1 teaspoon garlic powder

Instructions:

1. Set the oven to 350°F (175°C).
2. Cut the top off the bread and form a bowl.
3. Combine the spinach, cheese, artichoke, and garlic powder in a separate bowl.
4. Scoop the mixture into the bread bowl and bake for 15-20 minutes.

Vegan Bruschetta [84]

Servings: 2

Ingredients:

- 1 ciabatta
- 1 tablespoon red wine vinegar
- 2 tablespoons garlic chilli oil
- 1 tablespoon basil, chopped
- 3 medium tomatoes, chopped into quarters

Instructions:

1. Preheat the grill on a medium heat.
2. Slice the ciabatta in half lengthwise and cut in half crosswise.
3. Rub the oil into the bread and grill for about 3 minutes until golden brown.

4. Combine tomatoes, basil, red wine vinegar, and the leftover garlic chilli oil in a bowl. Add in salt and pepper if needed.
5. Top the grilled ciabatta with the tomato mixture and serve

Mini Vegan Pizza Bites [85]

Servings: 3

Ingredients:

- 1 large courgette, sliced in ¼ inch rounds
- 1 cup vegan cheese, grated
- 2 tablespoons pizza sauce
- Toppings of choice
- Seasonings like oregano or nutritional yeast

Instructions:

1. Set the oven to 450°F (230°C).
2. Place the courgette rounds on a greased baking sheet.
3. Top each round with pizza sauce, toppings, and seasonings of your choice and cover with cheese.
4. Bake for about 7-8 minutes and then grill for 5 minutes.

Vegan Cheese-Stuffed Jalapenos [86]

Servings: 6

Ingredients:

- 2 cups vegan cheddar cheese, grated
- 12 jalapeño peppers
- 1 cup vegan cream cheese
- ¼ cup breadcrumbs
- 1 teaspoon oregano

Instructions:

1. Set the oven to 400°F (200°C).
2. Cut jalapeño peppers in half lengthwise and remove the membrane and seeds.
3. In a bowl, combine the cream cheese, cheddar cheese, and oregano. Stuff each jalapeño pepper with the cheese mixture and top with breadcrumbs.
4. Bake for about 25 minutes.

Vegan Pesto Pinwheels [87]

Servings: 2

Ingredients:

- 2 large wraps
- 3-4 tablespoons tahini pesto
- 1 cup cherry tomatoes, diced
- 1 cup mushrooms, sautéed
- 1 cup baby spinach

Instructions:

1. Spread pesto over each wrap.
2. Layer in rows of mushrooms, baby spinach, and cherry tomatoes.
3. Roll it up and cut it into bite-sized pieces.

Vegan Onion Rings [88]

Servings: 25 onion rings

Ingredients:

- 3 onions
- 1¼ cups breadcrumbs
- ⅓ cup flour
- ⅔ cup aquafaba
- Spices of your choice

Instructions:

1. Preheat the oven to 355°F (180°C).
2. Cut the onions into rings.
3. Prepare three bowls. Place the flour in the first bowl, aquafaba in the second, and a mix of spices and breadcrumbs in the third bowl.
4. Line a baking tray with greaseproof baking paper.
5. Place the onion ring in the bowl and coat it with flour from both sides. Then, place them in aquafaba and then in breadcrumbs.
6. Once the onion ring is well coated, put it on the baking tray. Do the same with all the onion rings.
7. Bake for 15-18 minutes.

Vegan Guacamole Deviled Eggs [89]

Servings: 24

Ingredients:

- 1 ripe avocado
- 2 cups almond milk
- 2 teaspoons agar powder
- 1 tablespoon lime juice
- Spices of your choice

Instructions:

1. In a small saucepan, place the agar powder and almond milk. Whisk on a medium-high speed until the almond milk

begins to bubble. Reduce the heat and whisk for about 4 minutes.

2. Quickly pour the mixture into each cup of the cupcake baking tray.

3. Leave in the fridge for 30 minutes. Once firm, scoop a small half-circle from each "egg."

4. Blend the avocado, lime juice, and any seasonings you like (garlic powder, onion powder, smoked paprika, salt, etc.) until smooth.

5. Pipe mixture onto the egg with a star tip.

6. Sprinkle with spices of your choice.

Desserts and Treats

This collection of easy-to-make vegan dessert recipes will suit your lifestyle whether you're a busy student with not much time on your hands, or you're an experienced cook with plenty of free time. They are practical, easy to make, and won't break the bank.

Stuffed Dates with Almond Butter [90]

Servings: 12

Ingredients:

- 12 teaspoons almond butter
- 6 whole Medjool dates, sliced in half, pitted
- 12 whole raw almonds
- Hemp seeds
- Ground cinnamon

Instructions:

1. Stuff each half of the dates with almond butter.
2. Top with a raw almond and sprinkle with hemp seeds and cinnamon.

Vegan Watermelon Feta Skewer [91]

Servings: 4

Ingredients:

- 1 cup cubed vegan feta
- 2 cups cubed watermelon
- Balsamic dressing of choice
- Mint leaves
- Basil leaves

Instructions:

1. Thread a watermelon cube onto a skewer, followed by a mint leaf, a cube of feta and a basil leaf.
2. Drizzle skewers with your favourite balsamic dressing.

Vegan Caramelised Onion Tart [92]

Servings: 4

Ingredients:

- 3 onions, sliced
- 1 square puff pastry sheet dough
- 2 thyme sprigs
- 3 tablespoons balsamic glaze
- 6 tablespoons olive oil

Instructions:

1. Set the oven to 400°F (200°C).

2. Use a glass or cup to cut circles of puff pastry sheet dough.
3. Place the onion slices on parchment paper and top with balsamic glaze, olive oil, and thyme.
4. After turning them over, place the puff pastry circles on top of the onion slices.
5. Put pressure on the onion and use a fork to make holes.
6. Bake until golden for 40 minutes.

Vegan Chocolate Avocado Mousse [93]

Servings: 2

Ingredients:

- 1½ ripe avocados, halved and pitted
- 3 tablespoons maple syrup
- 3 tablespoons cocoa powder
- 1 teaspoon vanilla extract or paste
- A pinch of salt

Instructions:

1. Add all the ingredients to the food processor and blend until the mixture reaches the desired consistency.

Almond Butter Rice Krispie Treats [94]

Servings: 9-12

Ingredients:

- 3-4 cups brown rice cereal
- ½ teaspoon pumpkin spice
- 1 teaspoon vanilla extract
- ⅓ cup maple syrup
- ¾ cup almond butter

Instructions:

1. Mix maple syrup, almond butter, pumpkin spice, vanilla extract, and an optional pinch of salt in a microwave-safe bowl.

2. Microwave the mixture for 30 seconds, whisk, and repeat twice until the mixture becomes thicker in texture.
3. Slowly add in brown rice cereal.
4. Place the mixture into a small lined dish, flattening and slightly pressing down.
5. Leave in the fridge for 30 minutes.
6. Slice and serve.

Vegan Banana Ice Cream [(95)]

Servings: 2

Ingredients:

- 2 cups premade frozen banana slices
- ⅔ cup coconut milk
- ⅛ teaspoon vanilla extract
- 1 tablespoon maple syrup or agave syrup
- Pinch of salt

Instructions:

1. Place all the ingredients in a food processor and blend until creamy and smooth.
2. Pour the mixture into a freezer-tight dish and freeze for at least 4 hours.

Vegan Peanut Butter Chocolate Bars [(96)]

Servings: 16

Ingredients:

- ¾ cup peanut butter
- 1 cup powdered sugar or icing sugar
- 1 cup graham cracker crumbs
- ½ cup melted salted butter
- 1 cup dark chocolate chips

Instructions:

1. Line a square dish with baking paper.
2. In a bowl, combine all the ingredients except dark chocolate chips.
3. Pour the mixture into the container.
4. Melt dark chocolate chips and 2 tablespoons peanut butter. Spread the mixture over the base.
5. Leave in the fridge for about 1½ hours.
6. Cut into 16 squares and enjoy.

No-Bake Energy Bites [(97)]

Servings: 20

Ingredients:

- ¾ cup creamy peanut butter
- 2½ cups quick-cooking oats
- ¼ cup maple syrup
- 1 teaspoon vanilla extract

- ½ cup mini chocolate chips

Instructions:

1. In a bowl, combine all the ingredients and create one-inch balls.

Banana Oat Cookies [98]

Servings: 12

Ingredients:

- 2 cups old-fashioned oats
- 1 cup mashed bananas
- ⅓ cup dark chocolate chips
- 1 tablespoon maple syrup
- ½ cup peanut butter

Instructions:

1. Set the oven to 350°F (175°C).
2. In a bowl, combine all the ingredients to make dough.
3. Form balls of cookies and place them onto a baking tray lined with parchment paper. Press down each cookie so that it's ½ inch thick.
4. Bake until edges are golden brown for 10-12 minutes.

Berry Parfait with Nutty Granola [99]

Servings: 4

Ingredients:

- 1½ cups almond yoghurt
- 1½ cups granola
- 1 mango, peeled and cut into small cubes
- ½ cup berry chia jam
- Fresh mint leaves

Instructions:

1. Place a layer of granola into four serving glasses.
2. Then, place a few tablespoons of blueberry jam and yoghurt.
3. Garnish with mint leaves and freshly cut mango.

Coconut Bliss Balls [100]

Servings: 12 bites

Ingredients:

- 1 cup unsweetened flaked coconut
- ½ cup raw almonds
- ½ cup raw cashews
- ½ cup pitted Medjool dates
- 1 tablespoon unsweetened cocoa powder

Instructions:

1. Soak the dates in hot water for a few minutes.
2. Place them in a food processor and add the remaining ingredients.
3. Process until you get a dough-like ball.
4. Form 2-tablespoon-sized bliss balls and enjoy.

Chia Seed Coconut Pudding [101]

Servings: 4

Ingredients:

- 2⅓ cups light coconut milk
- ½ teaspoon pure vanilla extract
- 1 tablespoon maple syrup
- 5 tablespoons chia seeds
- Pinch of kosher salt

Instructions:

1. In a bowl, combine all the ingredients.
2. Cover and leave in the fridge overnight.
3. In the morning, portion into your dishes and add toppings of choice.

Vegan Coconut Macaroons ⁽¹⁰²⁾

Servings: 14

Ingredients:

- ½ cup full-fat coconut milk
- ⅓ cup and 1 tablespoon maple syrup
- 1¾ cups desiccated coconut
- ⅛ teaspoon fine salt
- 2 cups vegan dark chocolate

Instructions:

1. Preheat the oven to 320°F (160°C).
2. In a small pot, heat maple syrup on a low heat. Whisk in coconut milk when the syrup begins to bubble. Simmer for 2-3 minutes, stirring occasionally.
3. Add in salt and desiccated coconut. Form macaroons and bake for 20-24 minutes.
4. In a bowl, melt chocolate over a water bath and top each macaroon.
5. Serve and enjoy.

Vegan Berry Crumble [103]

Servings: 4

Ingredients:

- 1 cup granola
- 2 tablespoons lemon juice
- 1 tablespoon maple syrup
- 2 tablespoons toasted quinoa flour
- 4 cups frozen mixed berries

Instructions:

1. Set the oven to 350°F (175°C).
2. Combine all the ingredients except granola in a bowl and transfer into a baking dish.
3. Top with granola.
4. Bake until berries are bubbling, for 30-40 minutes.

Dark Chocolate-Dipped Strawberries [104]

Servings: 6

Ingredients:

- 1 cup vegan chocolate chips
- 2 cups strawberries
- 1 teaspoon coconut or olive oil
- Crushed nuts
- Coconut flakes

Instructions:

1. Melt chocolate chips with a double boiler on the stove or microwave.
2. Dip each strawberry into the chocolate and place on a baking sheet lined with greaseproof baking paper.
3. Add toppings like crushed nuts or coconut flakes.
4. Leave in the fridge until set.

Vegan Rice Pudding *(105)*

Servings: 4

Ingredients:

- 3 tablespoons coconut cream
- 2 teaspoons vanilla extract
- 3 tablespoons sugar; adjust to taste
- 2 cups unsweetened almond milk

- 5 tablespoons uncooked short-grain rice

Instructions:

1. Soak the rice in cold water for about 1 hour.
2. Combine the rice, milk, sugar, salt, and vanilla extract in a saucepan.
3. Bring to the boil and simmer on low heat for 15-17 minutes. Stir occasionally.
4. Remove from the heat and let it sit for 5 minutes.
5. Once the pudding is thick, stir in the coconut cream.
6. Let it cool for 30 minutes and serve.

Frozen Banana Bites [106]

Servings: 14

Ingredients:

- 2 tablespoons cacao
- 2 tablespoons crunchy peanut butter
- 3 overripe bananas
- ⅛ teaspoon salt
- ¼ teaspoon lemon juice

Instructions:

1. In a bowl, mix all the ingredients.
2. Pour the mixture into the silicone mini-cupcake moulds.
3. Place in the freezer for at least 6 hours or overnight.

Sweet Beverages

Pineapple Mint Green Smoothie [107]

Servings: 2-3

Ingredients:

- 1 cup cold water
- 10-15 mint leaves
- 2 heaping cups of pineapple
- 1 heaping cup of sliced English cucumber
- 1 cup fresh baby spinach

Instructions:

1. Place all the ingredients into a blender and process until smooth.

Homemade Almond Milk [108]

Servings: 3

Ingredients:

- 3 cups water
- 1 cup almonds, soaked overnight
- pinch cinnamon
- 1 teaspoon vanilla extract
- 2 Medjool dates, pitted

Instructions:

1. Blend all the ingredients in a blender until the liquid is smooth.
2. Use a nut milk bag to strain the milk.
3. Pour the almond milk into an airtight container and place in the fridge.

Watermelon Cucumber Cooler [109]

Servings: 4

Ingredients:

- 1 small/medium cucumber, peeled
- 4 heaping cups of peeled watermelon chunks
- 2 teaspoons grated ginger
- 3-5 mint leaves
- Juice of ½ to 1 lime

Instructions:

1. Blend all the ingredients until thoroughly smooth.

Berry Spinach Smoothie *(110)*

Servings: 2

Ingredients:

- ¼ cup rolled oats
- 1 banana
- 2 cups mixed berries, fresh or frozen
- 1 cup unsweetened vanilla almond milk
- 1 cup fresh spinach

Instructions:

1. Place all the ingredients into a blender and process until smooth.

Iced Matcha Latte [111]

Serving: 1

Ingredients:

- 2 tablespoons hot water
- 1 teaspoon matcha powder
- 1 tablespoon agave syrup
- 1 cup oat milk
- ¼ cup ice cubes

Instructions:

1. Mix the hot water and matcha powder in a bowl until it's fully dissolved.
2. Place ice in a glass and pour the milk on top.
3. Add the agave syrup and mix until it's dissolved.
4. Add the matcha mixture to the milk and stir well.

Vegan Hot Chocolate [112]

Servings: 1

Ingredients:

- 1½ tablespoons dairy-free semisweet chocolate
- 1 tablespoon unsweetened cocoa powder
- 1 cup unsweetened almond milk
- ⅛ teaspoon peppermint extract
- 1 tablespoon raw sugar

Instructions:

1. Pour almond milk into a big mug and microwave for 60 seconds.
2. Add cocoa powder, sweetener and chocolate and mix well to combine.
3. Microwave for 1-2 more minutes.
4. Add peppermint extract and enjoy.

Blueberry Lemonade [113]

Servings: 3

Ingredients:

- 1 cup water
- 1 cup freshly squeezed lemon juice
- 1 cup fresh blueberries
- 1 cup sugar
- Lots of ice cubes

Instructions:

1. In a saucepan, heat up sugar and water until sugar dissolves.
2. Add in fresh blueberries and cook for 3-4 minutes, mashing blueberries.
3. Strain the mixture and let it cool. Pour the mixture into a jug, add lemon juice and ice cubes.

Green Detox Smoothie *(114)*

Servings: 3

Ingredients:

- 1½ cups coconut water
- 1 cup frozen pineapple chunks
- 1 medium avocado
- 2 cups fresh spinach
- 2 teaspoons fresh ginger, grated

Instructions:

1. Place all the ingredients into a blender and process until smooth.

Conclusion

Entering a vegan lifestyle is a choice that aligns with your morals and values, and I hope this book has helped you to navigate your vegan experience through higher education.

You've learned how to prepare and cook plant-powered foods using only a few ingredients while keeping the food deliciously tasty and ensuring that your body gets the necessary nutrients to keep you healthy, strong, and mentally focused.

The aim of this book is to empower you and give you the knowledge needed to successfully navigate your college life to minimise the stress that can be put on your body due to restricted finances, long study hours, and convenience-focused eating.

You've learned about meal planning, shopping on a budget, and the easy way to navigate social events.

Recipes included in this book are easy, quick to prepare, and designed to give you an opportunity for self-care. They're completely suited to the lifestyle of a college student.

The breakfast recipes will help you kickstart your day, and the lunch recipes are nutrient-packed and easy to prepare.

Dinners are easy and convenient, and delicious snacks and desserts are treats to satisfy everyone's taste.

Keep this book handy and return to it whether you are in a rush and need to prepare a quick and simple meal or if you are looking for ideas for your weekly meal plan.

Embracing a plant-powered lifestyle is not only about the present; it's an investment in the future where you're leaving an imprint on the world in which well-being is the priority and animals are treated with kindness. It is not a destination but the continuation of making conscious choices about treating your body and the world with respect.

I wish you all the best on your journey to a plant-powered lifestyle and a lifetime of well-being.

Thank You

Thank you for reading *The 5 Ingredient Plant-Powered Cookbook for College Students.*

If you enjoyed reading this book and benefited from the recipes, insights, and guidance, please consider leaving a review on Amazon. Even if your review is only a few sentences long, it means the world to me.

By sharing your thoughts, you're helping other readers discover this book and benefit from the information I shared.

To join the mailing list, receive updates on future books, and receive information about health, weight loss, and nutrition, please go to bit.ly/silvana-signup.

About the Author

Silvana Siskov is the author of numerous books focusing on health, weight loss, and well-being. She is a dedicated health coach, counsellor, and nutritionist. Over the last two decades, she has focused her time and attention on helping her clients manage various problems, including weight loss, issues with confidence, stress, and other psychological and emotional issues. She has a deep-seated desire to help others and, through her work, has successfully done so.

When Silvana experienced her own health issues about 10 years ago, she found that focusing on self-care helped turn her health and life around. She started to feel full of energy and in a better place. By implementing certain lifestyle changes, she became confident that she could help others do the same, and by doing so, they could improve their health and well-being.

The power of a healthy lifestyle comes from within. By giving sound advice on a strong and balanced diet and focusing on the power of sleep, exercise, and self-care, Silvana has helped countless people overcome chronic stress conditions and other health issues that negatively affected their lives.

With Silvana's strong background in psychology and her combined working and personal experience, she has empathy and understanding for her clients, which helps her connect with them on a deeper level so they can make positive and successful changes in their lives.

More recently, Silvana's books have made a significant difference in her readers' lives, helping them with their weight loss issues, menopausal symptoms, emotional and binge eating, and generally having better health and improved well-being.

Helpful Resources

Books by Silvana Siskov:

- *Get Your Sparkle Back: 10 Steps to Weight Loss and Overcoming Emotional Eating.* This book is available on Amazon. Go to http://viewbook.at/sparkle.

- *Live Healthy on a Tight Schedule: 5 Easy Ways for Busy People to Develop Sustainable Habits Around Food, Exercise and Self-Care.* This book is available on Amazon. Go to http://viewbook.at/livehealthy.

- *Get Fit and Healthy in Your Own Home in 20 Minutes or Less: An Essential Daily Exercise Plan and Simple Meal Ideas to Lose Weight and Get the Body You Want.* This book is available on Amazon. Go to http://viewbook.at/get-fit.

- *Get Fit and Healthy on a Tight Schedule 2 Books in 1.* This book is available on Amazon. Go to http://viewbook.at/get-fit2books.

- *Beat Your Menopause Weight Gain: Balance Hormones, Stop Middle-Age Spread, Boost Your Health And Vitality.* This book is available on Amazon. Go to http://viewbook.at/beat-menopause.

- *Free Yourself From Hot Flushes and Night Sweats: The Essential Guide to a Happy And Healthy Menopause.* This book is available on Amazon. Go to http://viewbook.at/healthy-menopause.

- *Manage Your Menopause 2 Books in 1: How to Balance*

Hormones and Prevent Middle-Age Spread. This book is available on Amazon. Go to http://viewbook.at/manage-menopause.

- *Break the Binge Eating Cycle: Stop Self-Sabotage and Improve Your Relationship With Food.* This book is available on Amazon. Go to http://viewbook.at/breakthebinge.

- *Relaxation and Stress Management Made Simple: 7 Proven Strategies to Calm Your Mind, Stop Negative Thinking and Improve Your Life.* This book is available on Amazon. Go to http://viewbook.at/stressfree.

- *The 10 Day Sugar Detox Challenge: The Ultimate Guide to Reset the Brain, Eliminate Sugar Cravings, and Break Sugar Addiction to Burn Fat and Lose Weight (30 Anti-Inflammatory recipes Included).* This book is available on Amazon. Go to https://mybook.to/sugar/detox.

Free Mini-Courses:

- *Discover 10 Secrets of Successful Weight Loss*

- *This is How to Start Eating Less Sugar*

- *Learn How to Boost Your Energy – 11 Easy Ways*

- *Your Guide to a Happy and Healthy Menopause*

- *This is How to Lose Weight in Your 40s and Beyond*

Free Mini-Courses Available at www.silvanahealthandnutrition.com/course/.

To join the mailing list for updates on future books and to receive information about health, weight loss, and nutrition, please go to www.bit.ly/silvana-signup.

References

1. Sarfas, A. J., (2022). *How Many Animals Can You Save by Going Vegan?* The Humane League. https://thehumaneleague.org.uk/article/how-many-animals-can-you-save-by-going-vegan

2. Cassidy E. S., West P. C., Gerber J. S., Foley J. A., (2013). *Redefining agricultural yields: from tonnes to people nourished per hectare.* Environmental Research Letters; 8 (3): 034015 DOI: 10.1088/1748-9326/8/3/034015

3. The Simple Veganista, (2021). *Blueberry Banana Smoothie.* The Simple Veganista https://simple-veganista.com/cinnamon-blueberry-smoothie/#How To Make Blueberry Banana Smoothie

4. Hoffman, J., (2023). *Peanut Butter Chia Pudding.* Choosing Chia. https://choosingchia.com/peanut-butter-chia-pudding/

5. Flatout Recipes. *Spinach Veggie Wrap.* https://recipes.flatoutbread.com/recipes/spinach-veggie-wrap/

6. Healthy Liv, (2019). *Simple Peanut Butter Overnight Oats.* https://www.healthy-liv.com/peanut-butter-overnight-oats/

7. Michelle Blackwood, (2018). *Vegan Banana Oatmeal Pancakes.* Healthier Steps. https://healthiersteps.com/recipe/vegan-banana-oatmeal-pancakes/

8. *5 Ingredient Blueberry Protein Muffins.* Diabetes Food Hub. https://www.diabetesfoodhub.org/recipes/5-ingredient-blueberry-protein-muffins-a.html

9. Szcebel, C., (2021). *Healthy Peanut Butter Banana Cookies.* Nutrition in the Kitch. https://nutritioninthekitch.com/soft-chewy-banana-nut-butter-cookies-vegan-no-refined-sugars-gf-fave-five-friday-good-for-you-cookies/

10. Haun, B., (2022). *Vegan Chocolate Chip Pancakes.* Elephantastic Vegan. https://www.elephantasticvegan.com/vegan-chocolate-chip-pancakes/

11. *Easy Tofu Scramble with Spinach.* (2023). Bad to the Bowl. https://badtothebowl.com/tofu-scramble-with-spinach/#recipe

12. De Laurentiis, G., (2023). *Coconut Yogurt Parfaits.* Giadzy. https://giadzy.com/blogs/recipes/coconut-yogurt-parfaits

13. *Almond butter and berry breakfast toast,* (2023). New World. https://www.newworld.co.nz/recipes/breakfast/almond-butter-and-berry-breakfast-toast

14. *Cinnamon-Raisin Oatmeal.* Physicians Committee for Responsible Medicine. https://www.pcrm.org/good-nutrition/plant-based-diets/recipes/cinnamon-raisin-oatmeal

15. Friedlander, S., (2023). (2023). *Easy Mango Chia Pudding Recipe -Gluten-Free.* Delectable Food Life. https://delectablefoodlife.com/easy-mango-chia-pudding-recipe-gluten-free/#tasty-recipes-3813-jump-target

16. *Adams, A., Vegan Chocolate Peanut Butter Banana Smoothie.* (2022). The Spruce Eats. https://www.thespruceeats.com/vegan-chocolate-peanut-butter-banana-smoothie-1000994

17. *Blueberry Overnight Oats.* (2023). Flavor the Moments. https://flavorthemoments.com/blueberry-chia-overnight-oats/

18. *Easy Refried Bean Burrito (Vegan).* (2022). Veggies Don't Bite. https://www.veggiesdontbite.com/the-best-vegetarian-refried-bean-burrito-recipe/#recipe

19. *Chocolate Banana Protein Shake.* (2023). Mae's Menu. https://maesmenu.com/recipes/chocolate-banana-protein-shake/#recipe

20. *Five-Superfood Buddha Bowl*. Feed The Soul Blog. https://feedthesoulblog.com/five-superfood-buddha-bowl/

21. *Mediterranean Chickpea Salad*. Emilie Eats. https://www.emilieeats.com/mediterranean-chickpea-salad/#tasty-recipes-9657-jump-target

22. *5 Ingredient Superfood Quinoa Salad Bowl*. (2017). Two Raspberries. https://tworaspberries.com/5-ingredient-superfood-quinoa-salad-bowl/

23. *Hummus Veggie Wraps*. The Vegan Link. https://www.theveganlink.com/sides-recipes/hummus-veggie-wrap/#wprm-recipe-container-2031

24. Zavatsky, A., (2019). *Easy Vegan Chickpea Salad Sandwich Recipe – Only 5 Ingredients!* Vegan Runner Eats. Adventure in Vegan Living. https://www.veganrunnereats.com/810/chickpea-salad-sandwich/

25. *Mediterranean Rice Bowl*. (2021). Hurry The Food Up. https://hurrythefoodup.com/mediterranean-rice-bowl/

26. Overhiser, S., (2023). *Black Bean and Corn Salad*. A Couple Cooks. https://www.acouplecooks.com/black-bean-and-corn-salad/

27. Bernard, A., (2022). *Easy 5 Ingredient Chickpea Veggie Wraps*. Make It Dairy Free. https://makeitdairyfree.com/easy-5-ingredient-chickpea-veggie-wraps/#recipe

28. *Tomato Avocado Sandwich.* (2023). Allrecipes. https://www.allrecipes.com/recipe/247225/tomato-avocado-sandwich/

29. *5-Ingredient Mexican Quinoa.* (2020). Simply Quinoa. https://www.simplyquinoa.com/5-ingredient-mexican-quinoa/

30. *Classic Vegan Caesar Salad.* (2021). Simply Quinoa. https://www.simplyquinoa.com/ultimate-vegan-caesar-salad/

31. Snyder, S., (2019). *5 Ingredient Asian Peanut Noodles.* Dinner Then Dessert. https://dinnerthendessert.com/5-ingredient-asian-peanut-noodles/#wprm-recipe-container-11092

32. *5 Ingredient Vegetarian Sushi Bowl.* (2023). Nasoya. https://www.nasoya.com/recipe/5-ingredient-vegetarian-sushi-bowls/

33. Hale, K., (2023). *Vegan Mediterranean Couscous Salad.* The Cheeky Chickpea. https://thecheekychickpea.com/vegan-mediterranean-couscous-salad/#recipe

34. *Strawberry Fields Salad.* (2023). Yay Kosher. https://yaykosher.com/5-ingredient-strawberry-spinach-salad/

35. *Easiest Vegan Caprese Salad.* (2017). Salad Therapy. https://saladtherapy.com/magical-vegan-caprese-salad/#recipe

36. Wicman, M., *Hearty Lentil Soup (Vegan)*. The Mama Maven. https://www.themamamaven.com/hearty-5-ingredient-lentil-soup-vegan/

37. *Veggie Wraps with Hummus, Roasted Red Peppers and Spinach*. (2022). Robin Miller Cooks. https://robinmillercooks.com/f/veggie-wraps-with-hummus-roasted-red-peppers-and-spinach

38. Drosdovech, J., (2023). *Sweet Potato Black Bean Quesadillas*. Broke Bank Vegan. https://brokebankvegan.com/sweet-potato-black-bean-quesadillas/#recipe

39. Overhiser, S., *Vegan Pesto Pasta*. A Couple Cooks. https://www.acouplecooks.com/vegan-pesto-pasta/

40. *Brown Rice and Lentils*. Shane and Simple. https://shaneandsimple.com/brown-rice-and-lentils-one-pot/#tasty-recipes-19459-jump-target

41. *Teriyaki Tofu Stir Fry*. (2021). She Likes Food. https://www.shelikesfood.com/teriyaki-tofu-stir-fry-5-ingredient-trader-joes-series/

42. *Zucchini Noodles with Easy Tomato Sauce*. Mealgarden. https://www.mealgarden.com/recipe/zucchini-noodles-with-easy-tomato-sauce/

43. *5 Ingredient Vegan Black Bean Burger Recipe*. (2022). Bites of Wellness. https://bitesofwellness.com/5-ingredient-vegan-black-bean-burger-recipe/

44. *3-Ingredient Healthy Broccoli Alfredo (Dairy-Free!).* (2020). Liz Moody. https://www.lizmoody.com/3-ingredient-healthy-broccoli-alfredo-pasta-recipe-vegan/

45. *Sabrina Ghayour's Persian "Adassi" Lentil Stew.* (2017). Food52. https://food52.com/recipes/67723-sabrina-ghayour-s-persian-adassi-lentil-stew

46. *5-ingredient butternut squash soup.* Kitchen Stories. https://www.kitchenstories.com/en/recipes/5-ingredient-butternut-squash-soup

47. *Spaghetti Aglio E Olio – 5 Ingredient Pasta Recipe.* (2021). Chili in a Pod. https://chiliinapod.com/spaghetti-aglio-e-olio-5-ingredient-pasta-recipe/

48. *Baked BBQ Tofu.* (2022). Cozy Peach Kitchen. https://cozypeachkitchen.com/bbq-tofu/#recipe

49. *5-Ingredient Vegetarian Grain-Free Stuffed Peppers.* Pantreze. https://pantreze.com/vegetarian-grain-free-stuffed-peppers/#google_vignette

50. Ting, C., (2023). *5-Ingredient Creamy Tomato Curry.* https://chloeting.com/recipes/5-ingredient-creamy-tomato-lentil-curry#google_vignette

51. Gordon, A., (2023). *Vegan Roasted Vegetable Quinoa Bowl.* https://www.eatingbyelaine.com/vegan-roasted-vegetable-quinoa-bowl/#tasty-recipes-39607-jump-target

52. Victoria, Y., (2020). *5-Ingredient Vegan Fried Rice*. Wow, It's Veggie? https://wowitsveggie.com/vegan-fried-rice-recipe/

53. Mullins, B., (2020). *5-Ingredient Sweet Potato Curry*. Eating Bird Food. https://www.eatingbirdfood.com/5-ingredient-sweet-potato-curry/

54. *Spinach and Mushroom Risotto*. (2022). Bonapeti. https://bonapeti.com/recipes/r-230912-Spinach_and_Mushroom_Risotto

55. *McMinn, S., (2020). Zucchini Noodles with Pesto*. (2018). My Darling Vegan. https://www.mydarlingvegan.com/zucchini-noodles-with-pesto/

56. *Pytell, R., (2022). Buffalo Cauliflower Wings*. Strength and Sunshine. https://strengthandsunshine.com/buffalo-cauliflower-wings/#tasty-recipes-29260-jump-target

57. Minimalist Baker, *5-Ingredient Sweet Potato Black Bean Chili*. Minimalist Baker. https://minimalistbaker.com/5-ingredient-sweet-potato-black-bean-chili/

58. *Teriyaki Portobello Mushrooms*. (2019). An Imperfect Vegan. https://animperfectvegan.com/2019/05/25/teriyaki-portobello-mushrooms/

59. *5-Ingredient Perfect Guacamole*. (2015). Blissful Basil. https://www.blissfulbasil.com/5-ingredient-perfect-guacamole/#recipe

60. *Zucchini Fritters.* (2020). The GreenQuest. https://thegreenquest.org/zucchini-fritters/#wprm-recipe-container-1490

61. Cinnamon Toast Crunch Chickpeas. (2019). Veggiekins. https://veggiekinsblog.com/2019/09/09/cinnamon-toast-crunch-chickpeas/

62. Hackett, J., (2022). *Easy Vegan Spinach Dip.* The Spruce Eats. https://www.thespruceeats.com/easy-vegan-spinach-dip-recipe-3377724

63. *Asian Cucumber Carrot Slaw.* Kitchen Confidante. https://kitchenconfidante.com/asian-cucumber-carrot-slaw-recipe

64. *Vegan Popcorn.* (2021). Namely Marly. https://namelymarly.com/diy-microwave-popcorn-vegan-cheesy-popcorn-recipe/#wprm-recipe-container-21060

65. Hackett, J., (2021). *Baked Vegan Sweet Potato Fries.* The Spruce Eats. https://www.thespruceeats.com/low-fat-baked-sweet-potato-fries-3377377

66. Drosdovech, J., (23). *Mango Salsa.* Broke Bank Vegan. https://brokebankvegan.com/mango-pico-de-gallo/#recipe

67. Webster. K., (2022). *Roasted Garlic Hummus.* Healthy Seasonal Recipes. https://www.healthyseasonalrecipes.com/roasted-garlic-hummus/

68. Cheng, X., *Edamame with Sesame and Sea Salt*. Kitchen Stories. https://www.kitchenstories.com/en/recipes/edamame-with-sesame-and-sea-salt

69. Apple Slices with Almond Butter. (2023). Peapil Publishing. https://peapilpublishing.com/blogs/free-recipe-of-the-day/apple-slices-with-almond-butter

70. Whisking Mama, *Homemade Hummus with Veggies*. https://whiskingmama.com/homemade-hummus/#tasty-recipes-12456-jump-target

71. *Baked Tofu Bites*. (2018) Mindful Avocado. https://mindfulavocado.com/baked-tofu-nuggets/

72. *Cucumber Hummus Appetizers*. Simple and Savory. https://simpleandsavory.com/cucumber-hummus-appetizers/

73. *Cook, A., (2020). Spicy Roasted Almonds*. It's Not Complicated Recipes. https://itsnotcomplicatedrecipes.com/spicy-roasted-almonds/

74. Olson, S., (2023). *Crispy Roasted Chickpeas*. Healthy Seasonal Recipes. https://www.healthyseasonalrecipes.com/crispy-roasted-chickpeas/

75. *5-Minute Vegan Spring Rolls*. Shayna's Kitchen. https://shaynaskitchen.com/recipes/5-minute-vegan-spring-rolls/

76. *Oil-Free Sweet Potato Fries.* (2021). Nutriciously. https://nutriciously.com/sweet-potato-fries/

77. *Avocado Salsa.* (2023) Thriving Home. https://thrivinghomeblog.com/avocado-lime-salsa/

78. *Easy Baked Falafel Recipe.* (2023). Sweet Simple Vegan. https://sweetsimplevegan.com/homemade-baked-falafel/

79. Winn, E., *Healthy Spinach Artichoke Dip.* (2022). Real Simple Good. https://realsimplegood.com/easy-spinach-artichoke-dip/

80. *Vegan Asian Cucumber Salad.* Voach. https://voach.co/vegan-asian-cucumber-salad/#google_vignette

81. *Vegan Caprese Skewers with Balsamic Glaze.* (2021). That Vegan Babe. https://thatveganbabe.com/vegan-caprese-skewers/#recipe

82. *Mini Vegan Quiches.* (2021). WallFlower Kitchen. https://wallflowerkitchen.com/35-calorie-mini-vegan-quiches/

83. *Dairy-Free Spinach Dip in Pumpernickle Bread Bowl.* Nuts for Cheese. https://nutsforcheese.com/blogs/dairy-free-recipes/dairy-free-spinach-dip-in-pumpernickle-bread-bowl

84. Jones, T., (2020). *Five Minute, Five Ingredient Bruschetta.* Ty's Table. https://attystable.com/easy-tomato-bruschetta/#recipe

85. Breiner, D., (2023). *Zucchini Pizza Bites*. (2023). Danis Healthy Eats. https://danishealthyeats.com/zucchini-pizza-bites/

86. *Easy Vegan Jalapeño Poppers*. World of Vegan. https://www.worldofvegan.com/jalapeno-poppers/#wprm-recipe-container-121709

87. Perez, C., (2021). *Vegan Pesto Pinwheels*. Plant Based RD Blog. https://plantbasedrdblog.com/2021/03/vegan-pesto-pinwheels/#tasty-recipes-3939-jump-target

88. *Healthy Oven-Baked Vegan Onion Rings*. (2020). Bunny Mommy Cooks. https://bunnymommycooks.com/en/recipe/healthy-oven-baked-vegan-onion-rings/#wpurp-container-recipe-3614

89. *Avocado Guacamole Deviled Eggs*. Nouveauraw. https://nouveauraw.com/main-dishes/avocado-guacamole-deviled-eggs/

90. *Almond Stuffed Dates*. (2021). The Plant Based Palette. https://theplantbasedpalette.com/almond-stuffed-dates/

91. *Watermelon Feta Skewers*. Watermelon.org. https://www.watermelon.org/recipes/watermelon-feta-skewers/

92. Cohen, R., *5-Minute Upside Down Onion Tarts*. Home Cooks World. https://homecooksworld.com/vegan-caramelized-onion-tart/

93. *Vegan Chocolate Avocado Mousse.* (2022). Chocolates and Chai. https://www.chocolatesandchai.com/vegan-chocolate-avocado-mousse/

94. *Easy Almond Butter Rice Krispie Treats.* (2020). Veggiekins. https://veggiekinsblog.com/2020/10/19/almond-butter-rice-krispie-treats/

95. *Vegan Banana Ice Cream.* (2023). Delightful Mom Food. https://delightfulmomfood.com/vegan-banana-ice-cream-no-ice-crea/

96. *5 Ingredient Chocolate Peanut Butter Bars.* (2018). Recipe thin eats. https://www.recipetineats.com/5-ingredient-peanut-butter-chocolate-bars-no-bake/

97. Longley, L,. (2023). *Five Ingredient No Bake Energy Bites.* (2023). Simple Joy. https://www.simplejoy.com/five-ingredient-no-bake-energy-bites/

98. Lala, L., (2023). *Vegan Banana Oatmeal Cookies.* Yummy Tales of Tummy. https://yummytalesoftummy.com/5-ingredient-vegan-cookies/

99. *Perfect Vegan Breakfast Parfait.* (2022). Nutriciously. https://nutriciously.com/vegan-parfait/

100. Larson, J., *5-Ingredient Chocolate Coconut Bliss Balls.* (2018). Plays Well with Butter. https://playswellwithbutter.com/5-ingredient-chocolate-coconut-bliss-balls-energy-bites/

101. Clarke, E., (2023). *Coconut Chia Pudding*. Well Plated by Erin. https://www.wellplated.com/coconut-chia-pudding/

102. *Vegan Coconut Macaroons*. Lazy Cat Kitchen. https://www.lazycatkitchen.com/vegan-coconut-macaroons/#recipe-start

103. *5-Ingredient Mixed Berry Crumble*. (2020). Simply Quinoa. https://www.simplyquinoa.com/5-ingredient-mixed-berry-crumble/

104. Nunez. K., *(2021)*. *Vegan Chocolate Covered Strawberries*. Clean Green Simple. https://cleangreensimple.com/recipe/vegan-chocolate-covered-strawberries/#wprm-recipe-container-4763

105. Creamy Vegan Rice Pudding. (2023). Full of Plants. https://fullofplants.com/creamy-vegan-rice-pudding/

106. *Frozen Banana Bites*. (2015). One Green Planet. https://www.onegreenplanet.org/vegan-recipe/frozen-banana-bites/

107. *Cucumber Mint Pineapple Smoothie*. Yay! For Food. https://www.yayforfood.com/recipes/cucumber-mint-pineapple-smoothie/

108. *How to Make Almond Milk at Home*. (2023). Two Spoons. https://www.twospoons.ca/how-to-make-almond-milk-step-by-step-photos-video/

109. *Atlas, N., (2019). Watermelon-Cucumber Cooler.* The Vegan Atlas. https://theveganatlas.com/watermelon-cucumber-cooler/

110. *Spinach Berry Smoothie.* Shane and Simple. https://shaneandsimple.com/spinach-berry-smoothie/#tasty-recipes-18250-jump-target

111. *Iced Matcha Latte with Oat Milk.* (2023). Get Set Vegan. https://www.getsetvegan.com/iced-matcha-latte-with-oat-milk/

112. *5-Minute Vegan Hot Cocoa.* Minimalist Baker. https://minimalistbaker.com/5-minute-vegan-hot-cocoa/#wprm-recipe-container-36007

113. *Refreshing Blueberry Lemonade.* (2021). Curry Trail. https://www.currytrail.in/blueberry-lemonade/

114. Krampf, M., (2013). *Detox Smoothie.* Wholesome Yum. https://www.wholesomeyum.com/detox-smoothie/

115. All images in this book are sourced from www.shutterstock.com

Made in the USA
Monee, IL
11 March 2024